**You are a Child of God**

# You are a Child of God

## WALKING IN FAITH, FAVOR, AND A FUTURE THAT IS OUT OF THIS WORLD!

DR. J CALAWAY

InnerMission Publishing ● Hammond

You are a Child of God Copyright © 2018 by Dr. J Calaway. All Rights Reserved.

*To The Gate*

*This is in Honor of an incredible group of people*

*You Truly are Children of God!*

# Contents

|  |  |
|---|---|
| Acknowledgments | xiii |
| You are a Child of God Book Launch Team | xv |
| Bible Translations and Versions | xvii |
| Introduction | 1 |

## Part I. Purpose of Proclamation

Just Believe
*"And who can win this battle against the world?*     9
*Only those who Believe that Jesus is the Son of God"*
*1 John 5:1*

Proclamation
*"But the Lord stood with me and strengthened me,*     19
*so that through me the proclamation might be fully*
*accomplished..." 2 Timothy 4:17 (NASB)*

The Power of Today
    *"For God says, 'At just the right time, I heard you. On the day of salvation, I helped you. Indeed, the "right time" is now. Today is the day of salvation. 2 Corinthians 6:2*     27

The Role of a Child
    *"Everyone who believes that Jesus is the Christ is a child of God. And everyone who loves the Father loves his children." 1 John 5:1*     35

## Part II. Power of Proclamation

Mountain Moving Faith
    *"He replied, 'Because you have so little faith. I tell you the truth, if you have faith as small as a mustard seed, you can say to this mountain, 'Move from here to there' and it will move. Nothing will be impossible for you." Matthew 17:20*     45

Royal Favor
    *"For the LORD God is a sun and shield; the LORD bestows favor and honor; no good thing does he withhold from those whose walk is blameless." Psalm 84:11*     55

Cosmic Future
    *"So don't be so surprised when I tell you that you have to be 'born from above'—out of this world, so to speak." John 3:7 (MSG)*     65

Ancient Foundation
    *"All Scripture is inspired by God and is useful to teach us what is true and to make us realize what is wrong in our lives. It corrects us when we are wrong and teaches us to do what is right." 2 Timothy 3:16*     71

Surefooted ......................................................................... 81
*"He makes me as surefooted as a deer, enabling me to stand on mountain heights." Psalm 18:33*

Bold Words ....................................................................... 89
*"Words satisfy the mind as much as fruit does the stomach; good talk is as gratifying as a good harvest." Proverbs 18:20 (MSG)*

Divine Attitude ................................................................. 97
*"Your attitude should be the same that Christ Jesus had." Philippians 2:5*

Listen Up ......................................................................... 109
*Jesus replied, "But even more blessed are all who hear the word of God and put it into practice." Luke 11:28*

Just Do It! ....................................................................... 119
*"Try to please them all the time, not just when they are watching you. As slaves of Christ, do the will of God with all your heart." Ephesians 6:6*

Convicted Lifestyle ........................................................... 127
*"And He, when He comes, will convict the world concerning sin and righteousness and judgment..." (NASB) John 16:8*

Face the Challenge ........................................................... 133
*"Anyone who meets a testing challenge head-on and manages to stick it out is mighty fortunate. For such persons loyally in love with God, the reward is life and more life." James 1:12 (MSG)*

Changed for a Purpose .................................................... 141
*"Don't become so well-adjusted to your culture that you fit into it without even thinking. Instead, fix your attention on God. You'll be changed from the inside out. Romans 12:2 (MSG)*

## Part III. Practice of Proclamation

Name of Jesus
*"Therefore God exalted him to the highest place and gave him the name that is above every name, that at the name of Jesus every knee should bow, in heaven and on earth and under the earth." Philippians 2:9,10*     147

The Amen
*"For all of God's promises have been fulfilled in Christ with a resounding "Yes!" And through Christ, our "Amen" (which means "Yes") ascends to God for his glory." 2 Corinthians 1:20*     153

The Challenge
*The Ninety-Day Believer's Proclamation Challenge*     159

About The Author     167

Resources     169

Cover Design:  CoverDesignPro|Nathaniel Dasco

Photographer:  Melanie Gwen Photography|Melanie Latiak

# You are a Child of God Book Launch Team

A special thanks to those who committed to the launch and success of You Are A Child of God:

Patti Barns
Joe and Diana Behena
Bev Calaway
Nathan and Carly Calaway
Victoria DeBaun
Elizabeth De La Garza
Steve and Abbie Del Rio
Jennifer Eades
Nathan Elizalde
George Furgye
Clare Goss
Judi Hyvarinen
Cassia Iglesias
Ana Rodriguez-Klarich
John J. Klarich
Joanne "Bunny" Konkol
Eliu Lopez
Marissa Lopez
Cynthia Luna
Chris D. Lampkins
Theresa Lampkins
Betty Macon
Judi Mikalouski
Steve and Bonnie Neese
Jeff Newburg
Sophia Powers
Amy Phifer
Rosalva Robles
Victor and Antonia Roman Sr.
Monica Rubio
Jonathon and Victoria Shawver
Elizabeth Silva
Jim and Carrie Sutherland
Priscilla M. Toney
Dustin and Brittany Wells
The Scott Wells Family
Joyce Zavala-Calderon

# Bible Translations and Versions

The Believer's Proclamation is based on Scripture. Each statement of the proclamation has a corresponding verse in the Bible. The use of different scripture translations within the book is wide ranging. We have determined to use different translations and versions to better communicate our point.

The use of different translations and versions also helps the reader to better understand scripture and the overall transcendent message the Bible brings.

Therefore throughout the book the common translation used will be the New Living Translation. The use of other translations and versions will otherwise be noted.

# Introduction

"He who sees the truth, let him proclaim it, without asking who is for it or who is against it."—Henry George

"Let us all remember this: one cannot proclaim the Gospel of Jesus without the tangible witness of one's life."—Pope Francis

## Believer's Proclamation

The power of proclamation in your life has the potential to change the direction and destiny of your life. Once a proclamation has been made and a core belief has been declared, the possibilities are limitless. It is a line-in-the-sand moment in your life. You declare to the powers that be, what you truly believe. When you speak out what is in your heart, at the core of your belief, you place the enemy on notice. The Bible says you will speak whatever is in your heart (Luke 6:45). You declare war! You declare war on those things that try to limit, distract, detour, and destroy you. I believe when you proclaim who you are, what you have, and what you can do, nothing can stop you.

On July 7, 1776, George Washington received a letter from John

Hancock. In that letter, Mr. Hancock wrote, "...enclosed is the Declaration of Independence. Proclaim it from the front of the continental army as you see fit..." That one act of proclamation gave birth to a nation that has influenced the course of history for the past two and a half centuries.

That proclamation has been reproduced in every form possible. Many carry a small copy of the Declaration of Independence with them. Some have memorized it. Citizens of the United States teach it to their children, and their children teach it to their children. To US citizens, the Declaration of Independence, next to The Constitution, is the most important document of the nation.

Upon announcing the Declaration of Independence publicly, the Founding Fathers declared war on Great Britain It was a solid and profound decision. There was no going back from that point.

For the next seven years, those who proclaimed and believed in the Declaration fought for independence. Lives were lost, fortunes vanished, reputations tarnished, and property destroyed. However, in the end, a nation was forged, centered around a core belief of who they were and what they could do. My point is not to espouse the core beliefs of the United States here, but to show the potential of proclaiming your declaration of BELIEF.

The Believer's Proclamation is just that: a declaration of who you are, what you have, and what you can do. This is not a declaration of independence, but rather a proclamation of who you are and what you have in Christ. It is a declaration of our dependence on God and our interdependence on each other.

Let me pause here for just a moment to give you some background on how this proclamation came to be. I have spent many years in personal study and private time with God. I am a devoted Christ-follower and committed to influence as many people as I can to become Christ-followers as well.

I was raised in a pastor's home and am an eighth-generation minister. All I have known is involvement and leadership in the church. My passion is about people finding who they are in Christ. I am the Lead Pastor of a church and have been involved in church leadership for over three decades. My desire has been, and continues to be, guiding those around me into the most incredible, victorious adventure in following Jesus Christ.

My father and grandfather taught me that what I say is who I am. My identity and what I truly believe about myself and my God comes out in my words. So, as I grew up, I always understood that my words must match my core beliefs. Understanding the importance of proclaiming what I believe every day, I sat down to write a proclamation of who I am in Christ and what I can do. This began as a personal devotional and exercise of my private commitment to God. The proclamation flowed from my heart, to my pen, onto paper in less than fifteen minutes. For several days, I recited that proclamation.

The confidence and conviction that came to me each time I spoke the proclamation out loud was incredible. After a few days of proclaiming this declaration in my private time with God, I realized this was not just a few statements for my personal, private commitment. This was a proclamation of belief; a daily declaration for an entire group of people. I felt I was meant to share this proclamation with those who attend the church I lead.

The following Sunday, I asked those in attendance to read the proclamation with me:

> Today, I am a Child of God.
> I have Faith to move mountains,
> Favor from the King of Kings,
> And a Future that is out of this world.
> My Foundation is the Word of God.
> My Walk is sure.
> My Talk is confident.
> My Attitude is like Christ's.
> Today, I will Hear the word of God.
> Today, I will Do the will of God.
> Today, I will be Convicted, Challenged, and Changed
> In Jesus' Name—Amen!!!

Every Sunday since then, we have recited the Believer's Proclamation before any one of our preaching team shares the message. The results have been incredible. We have seen hundreds of individuals who have been discouraged, discontented, disconnected, or indebted begin to understand who they are in Christ.

A young man who was experiencing difficulty at his job walked into work one day, faced with the possibility of being fired. He opened his locker and, in the quietness of his mind, began to hear the words, "Today, I am a child of God...I have faith to move mountains..." He began to claim the promise that he was highly favored. He did not let his present circumstances distract him from who he was and what he could do. He walked confidently in the face of opposition and allowed the attitude of Christ to radiate from his countenance. Not only did he keep his job but he was promoted. Today, he is in management with that same company.

I don't want you to think this proclamation is just for a local pastor and his congregation. On the contrary, the Believer's Proclamation is a declaration for anyone who determines in their heart who they are in Christ and what God can do through them. The proclamation is based on scripture. Each statement has a corresponding verse of the Bible.

You can begin each day without any proclamation at all and let life hand you whatever it will. You can start your day with, "I am a child of God..." and lay the foundation for where you will go, how you will respond, and what you will do that day. If you start your day with, "I am not good enough... I don't have what it takes..." you also lay the foundation for where you will go, how you will respond, and what you will do. Both proclamations have outcomes. Which outcome do you want?

My prayer for you is that you will begin to live your life proclaiming what your Heavenly Father believes about you: "You are a child of God who has faith to move mountains, favor from the King of Kings, and a future that is out of this world." Each time we, as a church, declare the Believer's Proclamation together, we end by giving the person next to us a high-five, look them in the eye, and say, "I believe it for you too."

A woman, Laura, who attends our church, works in a local hospital as a nurse supervisor. She printed and framed the Believer's Proclamation and hung it on the wall by her desk. Every time someone enters her office, they see the words that begin, "Today, I am a child of God..." One day, she told me that she has many of her nurses come to her office at the beginning of their shift to verbally declare the proclamation before they make their rounds to care for patients.

Putting the Believer's Proclamation on the wall of her office came about because each time we spoke it in church we ended with , "I believe it for you too." She started believing the proclamation for her nurses. Now, those nurses are sharing the proclamation with their patients and believing it for them as well.

Over these next pages, you will be taken on a tour of the proclamation and what each part of it means. You will be shown how to claim each declaration as you begin to align yourself and your belief with what God believes about and declares over you. At the end of the book is a ninety-day Proclamation Challenge.

## The Challenge:

1. Memorize the Believer's Proclamation.
2. Commit to reciting it every morning for ninety days.
3. Complete the Believer's Proclamation Bible Study.
4. Memorize the corresponding Bible verse for each statement of the Believer's Proclamation.

I encourage you to do the challenge with your spouse, family, group of friends, co-workers, or other small group. Make it a ninety day commitment and see what God will do as you proclaim who you believe, who you are, and what you can do.

Begin to walk in the amazing blessing and power of the Believer's Proclamation!!! And never forget:

I believe it for you too!!!

PART I

# Purpose of Proclamation

*This Means War*

# Just Believe

"AND WHO CAN WIN THIS BATTLE AGAINST THE WORLD? ONLY THOSE WHO BELIEVE THAT JESUS IS THE SON OF GOD" 1 JOHN 5:1

"All I have seen teaches me to trust the Creator for all I have not seen." Ralph Waldo Emerson

On September 9, 1965, Admiral James B. Stockdale went missing. He was the highest-ranking officer in the US Armed Forces to be captured and had been shot down before. This was nothing new for Admiral Stockdale. Yet, what he was faced for the next seven and a half years would define his destiny. He had flown many missions over the Gulf of Tonkin and North Vietnam. On one occasion, he had to eject into the Gulf and wait to be rescued.

A mission to strike the Thanh Hóa Bridge had been scheduled. The weather was threatening and a mission delay was discussed. Finally, the green light was given by command, and Admiral

Stockdale climbed into his A-4 Skyhawk fighter jet to lead the aerial assault.

As the mission continued, the weather worsened, and those in charge made the decision to change rather than abort the mission altogether. During the assault on the new targets, Stockdale's fighter jet was hit and the admiral was forced to eject. In the midst of the firestorm, he landed in a small Vietnamese village.

Commander Foster, Stockdale's wingman, passed by to see if he'd landed safely and to track his location, only to witness the admiral being severely beaten by the villagers. There was nothing Commander Foster could do. Admiral Stockdale had been captured by the North Vietnamese and taken to the prisoner of war camp in Hanoi, which came to be known as the Hanoi Hilton, during the Vietnam War. For the next seven and a half years, Admiral Stockdale was a "tenant" of the "hotel."

Can you imagine being without eight Christmases, eight Thanksgivings, eight Independence Days, eight birthdays, and eight anniversaries? During his imprisonment, he missed weddings, funerals, kisses, hugs, school plays, days at the beach, vacations, promotions, births, teaching his children, and on and on goes the list of missings.

The things he didn't miss: seven and a half years of beatings, solitary confinement, torture, subpar food, and psychological warfare…he witnessed and experienced all of that. Stockdale did not miss the uncertainty of the condition of his family, the well-being of the soldiers he commanded, and the progress of the war. He had no reason to think he was ever going to get out of the situation he was in. There was no foundation on which to think he would ever see his wife again—except for the foundation of his belief.

Stockdale said in an interview with Jim Collins "I never doubted not only that I would get out, but also I would prevail in the end and turn this experience into the defining event of my life, in which, in retrospect, I would not trade."

You see, belief was that powerful for Stockdale. It turned what, for many, would be the most destructive event of their life into the defining event of his. He never stopped believing, having faith, and focusing on the fact that this, too, would pass. This level of belief is just as crucial to the believer in the effectiveness of the proclamation. It is a core ability to not allow the circumstances of the present to cloud the judgment of the future.

Some might look at this as hyper-faith or name it—claim it kind of living. While I believe it is important to verbally proclaim who you are and what you can do, there is also the need for you to be very clear about your current circumstances. Admiral Stockade continued to give insight to what he learned about belief and faith.

Collins asked Stockdale, "What prisoners did not make it out of Hanoi Hilton?"
Admiral Stockade responded, "Oh that's easy, the optimists. They were the ones who said, 'We're going to be out by Christmas.' And Christmas would come, and Christmas would go. They'd say, 'We're going to be out by Easter.' And Easter would come, and Easter would go. And then Thanksgiving, and then it would be Christmas again. They died of a broken heart."

Many have believed and fought for such ideas, concepts, and visions and never witnessed the accomplishment. William Wilberforce, the great English statesmen who fought to end slavery in Britain, died on July 29, 1833. The Slavery Abolition Act was signed on August 28, 1833. Wilberforce never saw his vision become reality. Abraham Lincoln, the sixteenth president of the United States, died before the end of the Civil War. He never saw the Union as he had believed it could be. The writer of Hebrews tells us that many gave their lives and fortunes for what they believed and had faith in, never to see it in their lifetimes (Hebrews 11).

> **Belief is not chained to a season or a time frame. Belief has no understanding of time.**

The power of this proclamation comes through your belief. Belief dictates behavior. When you truly believe something, when it is not just words, but belief, you will begin to act accordingly. What you truly believe in your deepest thoughts and mind is how you behave. If you do not truly believe the key in your pocket will open the door to your house, you will not even try. Yet, you have already opened the door to your house with that key on many occasions without even thinking about it. When your belief dictates, without thought, what it takes to open the door to your house, your actions become automatic.

How many times have you arrived at work, home, or the store and realized you didn't even know how you got there? You don't remember getting in the car, turning the key in the ignition, pulling out of the drive, stopping at the stoplight, turning into the parking lot, or walking through the door of the store. It was almost as if you were on autopilot. That is the power of belief. When your mind has accepted a certain belief, you will automatically begin to behave that way.

When a person says she believes she is a child of God but does not behave like a child of God, her proclamation is suspect. Being a child of God means you have accepted Jesus, God's Son, as the Leader of your life and the Savior of your soul. It is the same for everyone. There is no other way, or no other person, by which you can become a child of God. It is only through your acknowledging and believing in who Jesus is and what God has done. Being a child of God requires you to proclaim your belief.

## ABCs of Becoming a Child of God

Your belief is connected to the process of salvation in Christ Jesus—becoming a child of God. Without belief, you cannot be saved. It is impossible. The basic formula for salvation is:

A+B=C (A = Acknowledge) + (B = Belief) = (C = Child of God)

### Acknowledge

The first step in becoming a child of God is confessing or acknowledging with your mouth that Jesus is the Son of God. Confession, here, is to acknowledge, agree, declare, profess, and proclaim openly and freely. This level of confession is the first step to becoming a worshiper, one who praises and celebrates that which they are confessing.

Jesus said, "Therefore everyone who confesses Me before men, I will also confess him before My Father who is in heaven" (Matthew 10:33). The act of confession is a public declaring of your belief. When you confess that Jesus Christ is Lord, you are acknowledging you are not lord, you have sinned, and are in need of salvation.

Paul, in Romans 10:10, states that our confession leads to our salvation. John the Baptist proclaimed that we confess our sins. Christ and Paul admonished us to confess who Jesus is. Our public acknowledgment of Jesus as the Son of God.

## Believe

Romans 10:9, 10, says, "If you confess with your mouth...believe in your heart." If you acknowledge and believe in your heart that you will be saved, you will become a child of God. Many people simply look at this as a simple formula of a prayer in a church or with a friend. Their salvation becomes an event rather than a belief system.

Your belief system leads to confidence, conviction, and trust. Whoever you truly believe in is who you will trust. Without belief, you cannot trust. The reason many lack confidence is because they are weak in their beliefs. If you are easily swayed in your beliefs, you will have difficulty trusting and being confident.

Becoming a child of God is not an event. It is a lifestyle founded on acknowledging who Jesus Christ is, and your need of forgiveness for your sins, actions, and disbeliefs. This part of becoming a child of God is basic and simple. It is an act of the mind and mouth. You confess (acknowledge) with your mouth that Jesus Christ is the Son of God.

The next part of the equation is a little more in-depth. The Bible says that we are to believe in our heart. In other words, to get down to the very core of who and what you trust. When you believe in your heart that God raised Jesus from the dead, you place the very foundation of your life, belief system, actions, and confidence in God Himself.

Notice Paul—the writer of Romans and many other books in the Bible—did not say, if you believe in Jesus, the cross, or a certain doctrine, you will be saved. No. You have to believe in the ability of God. You have to believe that God is more powerful than death. You have to believe that God is the God of resurrection.

The Believer's Proclamation is not just a document to be recited to make you feel good each morning. The Believer's Proclamation is reinforcing what you believe about God, what God believes about you, and what you truly have confidence in. Your belief is the foundational component for the effectiveness of the proclamation. This is belief in your heart. The very core of your being. The word for heart here denotes the very center of all physical and spiritual life. Your heart is the very fountainhead of life.

When you believe something in your heart, that is the seat of your spiritual life. It is the seat from which come your thoughts, passions, desires, appetites, affections, purposes, and endeavors. While this kind of belief is not an intellectual belief, it is the foundation of intelligence, understanding, will, and character. What you believe in your heart affects your sensibilities, energies, vigor, and vitality.

Quite literally, your belief system will determine your force in this life. This may sound a little melodramatic, but listen to those who have achieved great things in life. There are stories of champions on the field, in the pool, on the court, in the boxing ring, CEOs and presidents. Some have degrees, others do not. Some have money, others do not. Some have talent, others are lacking. There is one common denominator between them all. They truly believe they could and would be champions, leaders, presidents, or CEOs. They believe they had what it took. Their belief did not come from their intellect, but from their core, their heart, and that affected how they thought, spoke, and acted.

It's not the words you proclaim that releases the power in your life. It is your belief, trust, and faith in God that releases resurrection power over, in, and through your life.

## Child

Once you have Acknowledged you fall short and need help and you Believe that Jesus Christ is the Son of God, you become a child of God. It is a basic act of confession and proclamation of belief. As a child of God all you do is win

**All You Do Is Win!!!**

I preached a sermon series entitled, "All I Do Is Win." The key scripture for the series was I John 5:4, 5, "For every child of God defeats this evil world, and we achieve this victory through our faith. And who can win this battle against the world? Only those who believe that Jesus is the Son of God." It is clear that we are victorious as long as we believe. When we believe, we can defeat the enemy, overcome the world, and be victorious over our flesh.

You may have been told as a child that you will never amount to anything. You may have more losses than wins. You may travel through more dark valleys than bright mountaintops. Remember, those are simply circumstances, events, or milestones that lead you to victory.

There is no room for the believer to lose, be defeated, or experience disaster. This may sound a bit too hyper-positive. Yet Jesus, in what would be considered the darkest day of His earthly life, won the greatest victory. It is said of Him, "who for the joy set before him, endured the cross..." (Hebrews . 12:2)

The foundation of the winning life as a child of God is belief. It is only those who believe that Jesus Christ is the Son of God who are children of God. I know you believe, and therefore your belief dictates your words. When devastating news comes your way, you simply say, "I believe the report of the Lord" (Isaiah 53:1) When your children turn to rebellion, you say, "I have trained them in the way they should go" (Prov. 22:6), and "I believe." When there is not enough money to pay the bills piling up, you say, "Seek first the kingdom and all these things will be added..." (Matt. 6:33), and "I believe."

Your behavior, words, and thoughts, when aligned with your belief that Jesus is the Son of God, turns any defeat, valley, or bad report into your greatest victory, triumph, and mountaintop experience!!! All you do is win!!! All you have is victory!!! All you are is a Champion!!! The Bible says we are moving from "Glory to Glory" (2 Corinthians 3:18). That means that every trial, difficulty, or struggle you go through transforms you to be more like Christ.

**Belief Dictates Behavior**

Belief dictates your behavior. You will read that statement many times in this book. I am convinced that whatever you believe is how you behave. Your belief system will eventually be the driving force of your daily life, in how you approach your marriage, finances, children, career, and community. Your belief will determine how you serve, how far you go in your career, what church you attend, what kind of friend you will be, and what level of commitment you will have.

Many will live contrary to their spoken word However, I am not talking about what you speak but what your core internal belief is. Your core internal belief is how you behave when the fire heats up, temptation rages, and external pressure mounts. What comes out in your actions and behavior at your breaking point is your true belief. Belief is the driving force of the Believer's Proclamation. You must have a strong driving force because when you proclaim, you declare war!

# Proclamation

## "BUT THE LORD STOOD WITH ME AND STRENGTHENED ME, SO THAT THROUGH ME THE PROCLAMATION MIGHT BE FULLY ACCOMPLISHED..." 2 TIMOTHY 4:17 (NASB)

"If you say something enough, you start to believe it.
Once you believe it, you become it."—Unknown

Make no mistake, we are at war. The Bible is very clear that there is an enemy force that is dispatched to overtake you. When you proclaim who you are and what you can do, you are sounding the alarm in the enemy's camp.

This war is not like any battle here on earth. That is why we do not fight the way the world fights. Paul writes, "we do not wage war like the world wages war...the weapons we fight with are not of this world. This war is a spiritual war. We do not fight against flesh and blood" (Ephesians 6:12),

We are constantly in a struggle with spiritual forces, our flesh, and the world systems. When you consistently proclaim who you are and what you can do, you are notifying the enemy forces that you are ready for battle and intend to win.

When I was young, I would sometimes do something that was less than smart. When I would make a mistake, say something wrong, or go somewhere that was not wise, I would simply say, "Man, I'm so dumb," or "I'm stupid." My dad would hear me and get very upset. He would look me in the eye with a very intense focus and say, "J, don't you ever say that again. You are not stupid. You are not dumb. Your actions or words may not have been the best, but don't call yourself stupid." I can hear those words ringing in my ears to this day. My father set the tone for who I was then, and who I am now. From time to time, I still have those thoughts, but as soon as they come, I hear the words of my dad: "You are not dumb."

To proclaim is important to the believer. Proclamation aligns the heart and the head and holds the believer accountable. When you proclaim something, you are giving notice that this is not only what you know, it is also what you believe. The proclamation is how you are going to act. When the act of proclamation is made from the heart, and on a consistent basis, it is at that moment your behavior begins to change.

You, as a Christ-follower, need to regularly proclaim who you are and what you believe. This proclamation is called the Believer's Proclamation because it is from someone who has made a decision and has authority. That is why every word of this proclamation is based on the Word of God. God is the One who has decreed these things, and now we simply align ourselves as believers to proclaim what He has declared. Realize that the words of this proclamation do not come from your authority or mine. They come from the very throne and mouth of the eternal Creator of all things, Jehovah.

## Source

Proclamation is giving verbal notice of something that has already been done, something that has already been decided. A proclamation is an order given from someone in authority. The Declaration of Independence was not a suggestion but a proclamation by those in authority.

In 1776, the authors of the Declaration of Independence were living under tyranny, oppression, and violence. The revolutionaries had tried for months, then years, to debate, discuss, and legislate their way out from under the bondage of the king. When the Patriots realized the king would never see reason, they made a decision. When we proclaim something, we are proclaiming what has already been decided by the authority.

The language in the Believer's Proclamation is strategically designed as a declaration. Notice there are no question marks. A proclamation is not something to be discussed, debated, or doubted. It is a decision from someone who is in authority (a King), and, as such, cannot be usurped, undermined, ignored, redefined, or questioned.

The questions of life can be overwhelming sometimes, without answers. Instead of living life with question marks, straighten those question marks out into exclamation points. Proclamations remove the questions in your life and point to the exclamation God has spoken over it. God does not have questions about your life. He knows very clearly, concisely, and confidently who you are, why you are here, and what you can and will accomplish. He had already written a proclamation of destiny over you before you were born (Ecclesiastes 6:10). He is not making this up as He goes along. He determined this from long ago.

This is the purpose, plan, and mission of Jesus Christ coming to the earth. His first message was to set the tone and plan for why He came. He stated, "I am here for two reasons to preach and to proclaim" (Luke 4:18). His message was of good news for those who lack; His proclamation was of release, recovery, and restoration. Yet the first words out of His mouth were to establish His authority and power. There is no strength to any proclamation without authority and the credentials to back it up. Children should not go into their home and proclaim how it is to be run. They are not the authority. The factory worker should not go into the president's office and demand the company function to his or her liking; he or she does not have that kind of authority. Many times we live under proclamations made by those who do not have authority over us.

The enemy declares that you are a failure, fearful, weak, and discouraged. Those around us tell us that we are not good enough, strong enough, or smart enough. They do not have the authority to make such proclamations. Think back to when you experienced people who had authority over you—a parent, teacher, supervisor, or spouse—and they said destructive things that have taken root in your life.

## Purpose

Proclamation means war. When George Washington read the

Declaration of Independence out loud in front of the Continental Army, he was declaring war. The Revolutionary War was a battle to determine who was going to be the authority over the colonies. When you proclaim, you publicly declare who has authority over your life. If you have been under the authority of fear, poverty, depression, sickness, disease, lust, failure, or lack, it is time to change authorities. Once you begin to proclaim who you are, do not become discouraged when it seems to be a battle. War is to be expected. The enemy is not going to allow you to quietly change allegiances. He is like a roaring lion who devours anything in his path. Declare your dependence as a child of God. The battle will begin, but you will be victorious. You are more than a conqueror in Christ Jesus!

While the enemy is like a roaring lion who devours, Christ is the Lion of Judah who breaks every chain. You may have been relegated to the chained slavery of depression, oppression, failure, generational curses, poverty, arrogance or pride, bitterness, hatred, perversion, or sexual immorality. You may believe that is all you are capable of or worth. It is time to switch lions. Move from being devoured every day to breakthrough, freedom, victory, and deliverance.

One of my favorite hymns growing up was "The Lion of Judah." The last line of the chorus was so incredible, I can still hear and see myself standing in a group of people and belting out that line loudly and confidently: "...the Lion of Judah shall break every chain, and give to us the victory again and again!"

Judah is one of the tribes of Israel. Judah means "praise." When you align yourself with the Lion of Judah, you no longer connect with the roar of the devoured...you will no longer accept defeat, discouragement, or discontentment. No, you have a roar of praise in you. The spirit of the Lion of Judah is in you. When you feel the chains of the enemy surrounding and imprisoning you, let out a roar of praise and watch those chains fall and shatter on the ground before you.

At this moment, you need to cut the declarations of those negative authorities off your life. You do not have to align yourself with those proclamations. When you proclaim I am afraid, I am a failure, I am stupid, I am sick, I am depressed, discouraged, defeated, I am a pervert, I don't have enough, I am _____ (fill in what you have previously declared), you choose what authority you will align yourself with. You choose the proclamations that will define your life. Just as the Founding Fathers of the United States had to declare independence from an oppressive authority, you must proclaim your dependence on your Heavenly Father.

**Proclaiming who you are every day creates an atmosphere in and around you.**

When you make a proclamation, whatever it is, your life will begin to follow that course. Choose today what proclamation will guide you, your family, your career, and your decisions. The Believer's Proclamation is not only for a release from oppression, but also a release into freedom, peace, love, prosperity, strength, courage, joy, acceptance, success, greatness, and faithfulness. The Believer's Proclamation is not simply designed to release you out of the pit but also to release you into the palace.

It is time to have the words of your heavenly Father in you. Every time you make a decision, you make it from the foundation of the proclamation of your Father and who He has called you to be. Every day, He says, "Today, I am your Father, you are my child."

Those words, when spoken in proclamation, can have a powerful impact on your life.

Proclamations set the boundaries in your life. Whatever you proclaim will be the limit of what you will do, say, or be. You cannot surpass that proclamation in your life. If you proclaim, "I am smart," you will start to make decisions as a smart person does. If you proclaim, "I am poor," you will make decisions according to poverty. If you proclaim, "I will never have enough," you will live in such a way. The power of proclamation in your life creates the road you will travel. Your life can be exactly what you proclaim it to be! And your life can be that today.

# The Power of Today

"FOR GOD SAYS, 'AT JUST THE RIGHT TIME, I HEARD YOU. ON THE DAY OF SALVATION, I HELPED YOU. INDEED, THE "RIGHT TIME" IS NOW. TODAY IS THE DAY OF SALVATION. 2 CORINTHIANS 6:2

"Seize the day. And put the least possible trust in tomorrow" —Horace

"Yesterday's the past, tomorrow's the future, but today is a gift. That's why it's called the present." —Bil Kean Cartoonist, The Family Circle

### Today, I Am...

We need to proclaim, every day, who we are, what we have, and what we do. The Believer's Proclamation starts with today, and several times it repeats "Today..." The word today is very important because it signifies when something is going to happen, and at what juncture in time something is going to be established. Have you ever heard someone say, "Someday I will…" or "Tomorrow I will…"? Well, you are not a child of God someday. You are a child of God today.

God did not say "Tomorrow is the day of salvation" or "Someday I will heal you." No, He said "today is the day of salvation (2 Corinthians 6:2 NLT)." Realize God is ready today, He is ready right now. The Bible states, "He is ready to settle this in your life right now" (Isaiah 1:18).

Today is your day for salvation from the penalty, presence, pleasure, and power of sin. Salvation for healing, deliverance, hope, forgiveness, restoration, reconciliation, and life—life abundantly. All this is for you today! You can stop reading right now and accept what He has for you this very moment. He is simply waiting for you to proclaim—today. If you have not committed your life and all you have to God through His Son Jesus Christ, consider doing that right now.

> **Simply say:**
>
> Lord, today I confess that Jesus Christ is the Son of the Living God, and I declare my belief that you raised Jesus from the dead. In Jesus's name, Amen.

## The Enemy of Proclamation

When you proclaim today, you are casting off procrastination. Procrastination is the enemy of proclamation. Procrastination says, "I have time, I'll do it tomorrow." Procrastination wants you to put off what you should do today. Jesus said, "No procrastination. No backward looks. You can't put God's kingdom off till tomorrow. Seize the day" (Luke 9:62 MSG). God does not want you to be afraid of what is coming next or to think you still have time. We are only given today. Make it count.

There has been a certain day set and it is called "Today" (Hebrews 4:7). It was set long ago and it is your day. No one can take that day from you. Your today is what you have to make a difference, to set the course of your life, and to lay aside all that is in yesterday.

*The pitfall of procrastination has so many spending their today regretting their yesterday. It is not the practice of those who proclaim today to wait for tomorrow.*

This is your fresh start. You cannot proclaim tomorrow; you can only proclaim today. King Solomon said don't brag (proclaim, declare) tomorrow because you have no idea what a day will bring (Prov. 27:1 MSG).

Why is today so important? Because today is all you have, nothing more, nothing less. Yesterday is gone and tomorrow is not here yet. Time is not like money; you cannot borrow tomorrow's time for today. Time is on a balanced budget. Time is on your side; you have today. But once that is gone, it is gone. You can only spend the time you have right now. There is no credit in time. Once a second, minute, hour, day (today), week, month, year, decade, or lifetime is gone, it is gone, and there is no getting it back.

Today is an equal opportunity employer for all. Today is twenty-four hours for everyone, no matter how much money, education, connections, or resources you have. It doesn't matter if you are black, white, live in the United States, Africa, Europe, or South America. You determine what today is for you. Every morning, you need to wake up and proclaim, "Today I am... I will do... I will be..." Then it is up to you to make that proclamation happen.

The beauty of today is, if it offers chaos, out-of-your-control conditions, or you simply fail to achieve your proclamation, you can start all over tomorrow when it becomes today. Just remember, it is not the habit of the productive to bank on starting over tomorrow, but to build on yesterday. The productive, successful leaders of today understand they have one shot at today, so it needs to count.

There is no boasting, banking, or focusing in tomorrow (Proverbs 27:1). The greatest enemy of today is the belief that you have tomorrow. The pitfall of procrastination has so many spending their today regretting their yesterday. It is not the practice of those who proclaim today to wait for tomorrow.

## God's today is not your today

Realize God's timing is perfect. Do not be impatient or discouraged. At just the right time, He will hear you (2 Corinthians 6:2). You just have to call on Him every day and not give up (Galatians 6:9). At the right time, suddenly, He will answer. Some might say, "I have been proclaiming every day and nothing has changed. I am still in the same place I have been." The point is not to proclaim in order to get something or become something. You are already a child of God. The point is that you walk in it today. When God hears that, He will answer. At just the right time, He will hear and answer. That is His Today, the day He answers, the day healing comes, the day you receive that promotion, the day you are blessed with that baby, the day your spouse or children are saved.

## The promise and provision in today

When you proclaim today, you are setting the parameter of the provision. When the children of Israel were wandering in the wilderness, they became very hungry. God provided a bread-like substance called manna. There would be so much manna it would look like snow on the ground. They could have gathered enough for the next forty days, even more. Yet God's command to His people in the wilderness was to pick up as much manna for each person in the household, not for the week or a few days, but only enough for that day. Every morning they would go out and fill their pots with manna. If there was any left over from that day, by the next morning the leftover manna would be rotten.

Don't rely on the provision you received last year, last month, last season, or even yesterday. Jesus teaches us the concept of daily provision in His prayer. When you proclaim, "Today, I am a Child of God..." you are matching your expectation to God's provision. You are proclaiming, "...give us this day our daily bread..." This is why you proclaim the Believer's Proclamation every day. It is a twenty-four-hour proclamation.

Put everything you have into today. Do not hold back. Leave everything else on the field, trust God will fill you up, and He will provide for tomorrow. God does not want His children to live with a scarcity mentality. He will provide for you each and every day. Living under a scarcity mentality says, "I have to store things up because I may not get another blessing, promotion, or paycheck." This is not to say we should not save or plan for the future. Proverbs tells us the wise save. Just do not let fear grip you and keep you from living and giving today. This is why many people have a problem being generous to others. They are afraid they will not get anymore, so they hoard what they have. It's a life based in fear. God does not expect you to hold back. He has never seen the righteous forsaken or His seed begging bread (Psalm 37:25).

Committing to today keeps you focused. It is very easy to rely on what happened yesterday or even many years ago. To fill up once a week in a worship setting with someone else giving you The Word is good and greatly needed. Yet a child of God needs provision every day. As you grow, you learn to find and feed yourself with the provision your Heavenly Father has for you each day.

David was anointed king long before he was made king of Israel. Yet that initial anointing and subsequent anointings were not sufficient to carry him through the years of his leadership. Those times when a priest anointed him were benchmarks of what God had called him to be. They were the markers he could refer back to, to remind him he was ordained by God to do what he was doing. The first anointing he received by Samuel was not designed to be effective enough to carry out the daily expectations of the king.

He said, "I exalt my horn and you anoint with fresh oil." Each day, David raised his horn and asked it to be filled with fresh oil. Each time you say, "Today I am a child of God," you are proclaiming a fresh anointing for that day.

When you proclaim, "Today..." you are setting the parameters for the promise. You are saying I want it today; yesterday's anointing is done and tomorrow's is not for today. It reminds you that every day you raise your horn and expect God to fill it.

**Trust Today**

You don't need clarity; you need trust... That is the answer John

Kavanaugh, a well-known Jesuit priest, received from Mother Teresa when he asked her to pray for him to receive clarity. He had spent his life studying ethics and wanted his life to make a difference. Kavanaugh viewed Mother Teresa as someone who had great clarity in her life and knew the answer to every problem. She stated, "I have never had clarity; what I have always had is trust. So I will pray that you trust God."

Too many times, we seek God for the answers, never realizing He is the answer. When you wake up each morning, put your trust in God to open the doors and opportunities today. You do not need to know all the details, or have clarity of what will happen in the future. There is a temptation to have proven trust. In other words, you trust God because He has provided something already. I have heard many people proclaim, "God, if you heal me, I will serve you for the rest of my life," "if you save my marriage, I will go to church every Sunday," or "if you save my kids, I will trust you." It doesn't work that way.

Each morning, when I wake up, I have a set routine. It grounds me and sets the tone and boundary for the day. I choose to determine my day. I encourage you to set a routine and follow it. Include the Believer's Proclamation as part of your routine and watch your days become more productive than you can possibly imagine.

## Determine Your Day

Do you have trouble starting your day? How you start it will determine the way the rest of your day proceeds. I have found three steps to starting my day beneficial for many years.
Spiritual

Spend the first part of your day in renewing your spirit. Take some time praying, reading scripture, and allowing God to prepare you for the rest. It is important to do this first thing in the morning, because you do not know what your day will bring. You may not get another chance to get some time alone to be with God.

## Physical

This is an important component of starting your day. Physical exercise gives you energy and stamina for the rigors of the day. Eating a healthy breakfast each morning will curb sluggishness. Remember to keep your exercise and eating habits aligned with your physical abilities. You may not be able to lift weights, run miles, or eat certain foods, but you can do something.
Strategical

Take time each morning to review your calendar and set goals for what you want to accomplish that day. Not days from now or life goals before you die, but simple steps to make your day productive. This will prepare you for any meetings, assignments, or projects you may have.
Remember, you only have today. Tomorrow isn't a sure thing and yesterday is sealed in history. Make today count for those around you and for those who come tomorrow.

As you learn that today has promise and power, you will begin to take on the personality, speech, actions, and the walk of a child of God. Do not become discouraged but determined to be the child God has called you to be.

# The Role of a Child

"EVERYONE WHO BELIEVES THAT JESUS IS THE CHRIST IS A CHILD OF GOD. AND EVERYONE WHO LOVES THE FATHER LOVES HIS CHILDREN." 1 JOHN 5:1

"As a child of God, I am greater than anything that can happen to me." —A.P.J. Abdul Kalam—Former President of India

## Today I am a Child of God

"Everyone who believes that Jesus is the Christ is a child of God. And everyone who loves the Father loves his children. We know we love God's children if we love God and obey His commandments. Loving God means keeping His commandments, and His commandments are not burdensome. For every child of God defeats this evil world by trusting Christ to give the victory. And the ones who win this battle against the world are the ones who believe that Jesus is the Son of God". (1 John 5:1-5)

Being a child of God is very special. This passage of scripture is a formula for accomplishing that. There are four components:

1. Belief
2. Love
3. Obedience
4. Trust

Every morning, God proclaims over you, "Today, I am your Father" (Psalm 2:7). As He proclaims who He is, you in turn proclaim who you are —"I am a child of God!" Being His child brings incredible blessings, guidance, gifts, protection, inheritances, wealth, and health. He asks, "What do you want? Name it—it is yours according to my incredible riches and glory" (Psalm 2:7).

**Your Father protects you**

When I was a kid, I got into a fight with a bully. He knocked me off my bike when I wasn't looking, and when I got home, my dad saw my torn shirt and bruised face. He didn't ask what happened, or who did this. He simply got up and took me and my bike to the park. He walked up to the kid who had done this, grabbed him by the collar, and marched him to his father. My dad explained what had happened and then looked at the kid and said, "Don't ever touch my son again." I realized something that day. My dad saw more than I thought he did. He had my back.

You might be thinking, "That's great for you, but I don't have a dad who has my back." Yes, you do, and He told you this morning, "Today, I am your Father." Were you listening? Did you hear it? "You are my child. Today I am your father; what do you need? I am here to provide." His name is Jehovah Jireh (Your Provider). You will never stay hungry, thirsty, or naked. You will no longer live in shame. Your shame is undone and your enemies will fall at your feet."

## Your Father persuades you

How do you know you are a child of God? Simply by believing that Jesus Christ is the Son of God; that Jesus is the Christ. This is the incredible message of God—that you should not harden your heart and turn away from Him (Hebrews 4:7). God wants to be your Father and you His son or daughter. All you have to do is simply believe in Him.

When you believe in Jesus Christ, a power that is not of this world comes into your life. You will be able to face all that the world and the devil can throw at you. Being a child of God does not mean you will never face death, destruction, discouragement, depression, temptation, betrayal, failure, or fear. Being a child of God means you have a power that can face anything, prevail, persevere, and be victorious in this life and the life to come.

## Believe What?

To be a child of God, you must believe that Jesus is the Christ. We have already discussed the power and need for belief in your life, so I won't spend too much time on it here. What is important in your life is what you believe. Realize you can believe anything, even if it is wrong. You can be sincere in your belief, but be sincerely wrong. The Apostle John states in 1 John 5:1, you must believe that Jesus is the Christ in order to be a child of God. We are adopted as sons and daughters of God when we believe Jesus is the Son of God. That is the prerequisite. There is no other belief that will get you the adoption. You can proclaim to be God's child, you can believe that we are all God's children, but John is very clear: The only way for you to become a child of God is to fully believe Jesus is the Christ. That Jesus is the Messiah prophesied by all the prophets.

## Love Who?

To be a child of God, you must love God's children. 1 John 3:10 says, "This is how we know who the children of God are and who the children of the devil are: 'Anyone who does not do what is right is not a child of God; nor is anyone who does not love his brother.'" Belief dictates your behavior, as we have already discussed. When you proclaim you are a child of God, you say, "I will behave like Christ behaves." This is why it is impossible to be a child of God and behave like the world (1 John 3:10). Your core belief will dictate how you live. Your Father expects you to act a certain way, just as you expect your children to act a certain way.

Loving God's children is the key to loving God. If you are truly a child of God, you have a mandate to love His children. If we don't love one another, we cannot call ourselves children of God. Again, John wrote in his first letter, "This is how we know who the children of God are...nor is anyone who does not love his brother" (1 John 3:10).

When questioned by the religious leaders of His time, Jesus told us how important it is to love one another. The leaders asked Jesus, "What is the greatest commandment?" Jesus replied, "The greatest commandment is this, to love the Lord your God with all your heart..." (Matthew 22:37).

Then Jesus said something I think is very shocking. The leaders asked for the greatest commandment, and Jesus wanted us to understand the priority of loving one another.

Loving God is simple, and this answer was expected from the Messiah, but then He went further. Jesus said the second is equal to it (the first) to love your neighbor as your self" (Matt 22:39). What was amazing, is Jesus was quoting Leviticus 19:18. He goes on to say, "All the Law and Prophets hang on these two commandments." In other words, Jesus put our vertical relationship with God equal to our horizontal relationship with one another.

All the Law and the Prophets encompassed the entire Old Testament. Jesus was saying that everything in the Old Testament can be connected to those two commandments.

Look at the ten commandments, the cornerstone of the Law of God. In Exodus 20, God gives a list of ten rules for us to live by. Most governments in the world established laws that are based on these foundations of human conduct.

1. No other God
2. No idols
3. Do not use the Lord's Name in vain
4. Remember the Sabbath
5. Honor your father and mother
6. Do not murder
7. Do not commit adultery
8. Do not steal
9. Do not lie
10. Do not covet

Remember, Jesus said the greatest commandment is to love the Lord with all your heart, soul, strength, and mind.

Commandments one through four all deal with our response to God. Jesus also said, "The second is equal to it, to love you neighbor as your self." Commandments five through ten deal with our response to one another. Jesus fulfilled what had been established from the beginning. Four "loving God" commandments to six "loving one another" commandments.

You do the math. Everything hangs on our treatment of one another. If we don't forgive, we will not be forgiven (Mark 11:26). If we say we love God and hate our brother, we are considered liars (1 John 3:14, 15). If we do not love those around us, we will never be a child of God.

## Obey

To be a child of God, you must love God and obey His commandments. Loving and obeying the commandments of God is all about being free. We obey because we love Him so much. The freedom of obeying and honoring is seen in 2 Timothy 2:4: "No soldier in active service entangles himself in the affairs of everyday life, so that he may please the one who enlisted him as a soldier."

The true child of God follows the orders of the commander, to please the one who enlisted him or her. If we are only to obey our Father because we are trying to be His child, we are missing the point. God has already adopted us and nothing can change that. So every action of love we manifest toward Him through obedience is not out of obligation, but an undying love and thanksgiving for who He is.

To understand the power of obeying, we can look at David and Jesus. David is known as a man after God's own heart. He loved the Lord and obeyed Him all his life. He didn't do it perfectly, and in those times he had to repent, and he did. With all the mistakes David made, he still is known as a man after God's own heart. It is said of David, he did what God told him to do. Yet Jesus was also one after His Father's heart. He did all His Father told him to do. On many occasions, He would pray simply to let those who were witnessing the event know He was about His Father's business and was from His Father (John 11:40-44).

When we compare Jesus with David, there is also the same love and obedience. Yet there is one difference. The Bible says Jesus did what His Father told Him to do when He told Him to do it. The key to love and obedience to God is doing what He says when He says to do it. Not when you have enough money, enough time, enough help, enough courage, but when He says to do it. The key to being a child of God is simple: pray and obey. What you hear, you do. It is that simple.

## Trust

To be a child of God, you must trust Christ. The true sign of trusting Jesus is obeying Him. Trust is displayed in the way you think. When you trust someone, you have a foundational belief in them. To be true, you are persuaded and have confidence in them. You trust they will not intentionally harm you or lead you in the wrong way.

Throughout our lives, we are tested in many ways. Each test is for one purpose: to see if we trust. If you do not trust anyone or anything, you will end up lonely and bitter. The key to being a child of God is trust. You may have been in a group in which they did a trust test: someone stands on a chair or on an elevated platform and falls backward, and those under them catch them. It is harder to do than it looks.

A baby is born with only two fears: the fear of falling and the fear of loud noises. The trust test confronts the basic fear of falling. You have to fight the very nature you were born with. The Bible says we were also born with a bend or desire away from the things of God. Just like the trust test, in falling backward and completely trusting those around you to catch you, you have to fight to overcome your natural desire not to do the things Christ calls you to do. It is complete and total trust in Jesus.

If there is no trust, there is constant questioning. For example, if a wife does not trust her husband, every time he is late, even if he calls to inform her he will be late, she will interrogate him, question him, and check up on him. He can explain until he is blue in the face why he was detained. He may have the proof, and yet, if there is no trust, no matter what he does or says, she will not believe him. Or vice versa, if the husband does not trust his wife the same applies. This is why so many people can listen to sermons, read the Bible, go to church, and yet never fully activate their life in Christ; they do not trust Him. Jesus can show them miracles, prove who He is over and over again, send sign after sign, and yet, just like the husband who could prove where he was, there is nothing Jesus can do to convince. Trust is the sign of a child of God

To believe that Jesus is the Son of God means you will win the battle against the world. Don't give up in your fight. Don't quit in your progress. God expects you to keep moving forward, to keep pressing on, to keep trusting, no matter what.

PART II

# Power of Proclamation

*Belief Dictates Behavior*

# Mountain Moving Faith

"HE REPLIED, 'BECAUSE YOU HAVE SO LITTLE FAITH. I TELL YOU THE TRUTH, IF YOU HAVE FAITH AS SMALL AS A MUSTARD SEED, YOU CAN SAY TO THIS MOUNTAIN, 'MOVE FROM HERE TO THERE' AND IT WILL MOVE. NOTHING WILL BE IMPOSSIBLE FOR YOU."
MATTHEW 17:20

"Faith is taking the first step even when you don't see the whole staircase."  Martin Luther King Jr.

### I have faith to move mountains

A child of God operates in faith. The kind of faith that moves the hand of God. All throughout scripture we see God is moved by our faith. Without faith it is impossible to please Him. (Hebrews

11:6) Jesus was astonished by the faith of the centurion who accepted Jesus' word above His action. (Luke 7:1:10). He had the kind of faith that Jesus had not seen in all of Israel, *Mountain Moving Faith.*

## Faith Activates

Faith is the activator of God. Without it, we cannot please Him (Hebrews 11:6), and we cannot expect anything from Him (James 1:5-7). Faith in God is crucial to the believer's life. Yet it is so easy to let faith fall, to let doubt storm in. Proclaiming faith on a daily basis is important to the believer because, if you are not proclaiming faith, you are proclaiming doubt. You may be sick, discouraged, or overwhelmed, yet when you proclaim faith, it pushes those things to the side, and your faith becomes the central part of your day. Faith must be present for you to hear the Word of God.

Faith not only activates God, it also activates the believer. Without faith, all you have is fear and doubt. God so wants to bless you and guide you along the most incredible adventure. Yet if you do not have the faith to step out of the boat, as the Apostle Peter did, you will be relegated to the limits of your doubt and fear. God wants so much more for you. Doubt and fear limit God. You cannot expect anything from God if you approach with doubt.

## Faith Determines

Faith determines your conviction. What you have faith in, is what you will be convinced of. Faith is

> Doubt is the enemy of faith and fear is its by-product.

a strong, welcome conviction that Jesus can and will do what He says He will do. Our faith is the foundation of our character and our reliability. Someone of faith is said to be faithful, meaning he is reliable. Without faith, you cannot be trustworthy. There is nothing to stand on, plant in, or grow with.

When you doubt, you begin to question everything. There is nothing wrong with asking questions. But there is a big difference between asking questions and questioning. When the angel appeared to Mary to let her know she was going to have a baby and call Him Jesus, she asked the question, "How can this be, I have never been with a man?" Mary's question was from faith in who she was talking to. She wanted to know what to expect next.

When the angel appeared to Zechariah, John the Baptist's father, he questioned the angel, "How can I be sure of this?" Two questions, but each from a different perspective. Zechariah's question came from a place of doubt in whom he was talking to. He couldn't get his mind around the fact that he, and especially his wife, were past childbearing years. He needed to know the end before he accepted the assignment.

**He could not grasp the fact that God was bigger than biology.**

Don't approach life like Zechariah, always questioning the Word from God in your life. When Zechariah questioned the authority of the Messenger, the result was that he lost his voice for a season of time. Your voice is who you are. It is your influence, your message, your identity. When the angel took Zechariah's voice away, he was in essence saying *I'm taking away your influence.*

A child of God has no business living with doubt. Zechariah was a priest. He was in the order of leadership for the worship and positioned in a place to hear God. Yet even at his level of leadership, he operated with doubt. God will only let you live to a certain level with your doubt before he challenges it and expects a greater level of faith.

Be curious like Mary. Be expectant like Mary. Be joyful and exuberant like Mary. Sing a song of praise, dance a dance of celebration, shout a shout of triumph. Then you will become an avenue for Jesus to become real in others' lives.

**Doubt will destroy your message, take away your voice, and tarnish your influence.**

Faith to move mountains is not a proclamation of a large amount of faith. Jesus said if you have just a grain of a mustard seed of faith, you can move mountains. In other words, build on what faith you have. You might say, "J. you do not understand, I have no faith." That is simply not true. Everyone has faith. The Bible states that each has been given a measure of faith (Romans 12:3).

Don't wish for more faith; enact the amount of faith you have been given. It seems some have been given more than others. Have you ever met someone who seems to be able to just believe and have faith in the biggest things? Or another can give large amounts of money or possessions and God pours out more on them? You may feel that you don't have enough faith to do that.

But remember, you have a measure of faith. You can have faith for things that others cannot. You may have faith for a family member, co-worker, or neighbor that others have given up on. That is your measure of faith. You may have faith for a community, a group, or a culture for which others feel there is no hope. Realize, that is your measure of faith. Your measure of faith is through the grace given to you by the Holy Spirit. Don't look to others to enact their faith on your behalf until you have enacted the faith within you.

Faith to move mountains is not a proclamation of pride or a boast. It is simply a declaration that at the very least, you have been given the smallest amount of faith. That seed of faith, so you can move mountains. Can you imagine, Jesus said that even the smallest seed is enough to move mountains out of your way? Mountain-moving faith is just the starting point. Mountain-moving faith is the baseline of the faith you have. As you exercise your faith, it will grow and become stronger.

Jesus places a high priority on faith. It is impossible to please God without it, as I noted before. There were times when Jesus would be frustrated with His disciples and the people around him, usually because of their lack of faith. On one particular occasion, He asked, how long He would have to put up with them (Matthew 17:17). Faith is a serious matter to God.

### Say it out loud—"I have faith to move mountains!"

Faith is not something you just give lip service to. This is not a simple hocus-pocus, abracadabra mystical mantra. There are three tests you must face and pass to see mountain-moving faith in your life. Jesus had to face these same three tests while He was going to the cross:

> **Faith is a lifestyle of sacrifice and stamina.**

- The test of deep disappointment.
- The test of standing alone.
- The test of trusting God no matter what.

## Test of Deep Disappointment

When Jesus heard Peter deny Him three times on the night He was betrayed, Jesus realized His closest friend and follower had turned his back on Him. The pain of rejection and abandonment is so real when you live the mountain-moving faith life. There will be those who refuse to go with you or follow you. Many times, it will be those who are closest to you. Do not let that persuade you to give up your faith. You must press on. Do not let the disappointment linger, because disappointment leads to discouragement and discouragement leads to despair.

## Test of Standing Alone

When Jesus was in the Garden after being in the Upper Room with His disciples, He went to pray and asked them to pray with Him. On three different occasions, He caught His disciples asleep. Jesus was all alone. Even though there were many around Him, He had to face the cross and the grave alone. When you face a mountain-moving faith circumstance, there will be times you have to face it all alone. There will be no one beside you.

Many years ago, my wife, Vicki, and I were sitting in my Ordination service. The speaker asked us to hold our spouse's hand. He told us that throughout life, we will walk together, build together, minister together. I was feeling very secure and confident as I held Vicki's hand. At one point, the minister told us to let go of our spouse's hand as he painted the picture of a field. The minister continued his Illustration: "You will have to walk through a field all by yourself." You will have to make a decision, launch a business, start a project, have to take a stand alone. Your spouse will be on the other side of the field, cheering you on. Your friends, colleagues, family will be there encouraging you, but you will have to walk the field alone. Making it through your field will give you the ability to succeed no matter who stays or who goes with you.

## Test of Trusting God No Matter What

I find it very interesting that we see the picture of God, our Heavenly Father, turning His back on Jesus while on the cross, Jesus, in a desperate cry, asked God why He had forsaken Him. Can you imagine the feeling of complete forsakenness at the culmination of your purpose? There will be times when it looks like total defeat and failure. It is at those times when you must trust God no matter what it looks, sounds, or feels like. Mountain-moving faith does not rely on our senses, but rather focuses on total trust in God.

## To have faith you must be willing to:

### Risk

What if this doesn't work? What if...? What if...? What if...? Every day is filled with "What ifs." The Bible tells us not to look at the circumstances around us (Ecclesiastes 11:4-6). The farmer who waits until perfect weather and watches every cloud will never harvest. The husband and wife who wait for the perfect time for a child to come will never give birth. The one who isn't willing to risk will never accomplish anything. There is a fine line between risk and foolishness. Remember, God said to plant your seed in the morning and go to work. You do not know what will come about in any of your activities, but just maybe, all your planting and hard work will prosper. That is up to God.

## To have faith you must be willing to:

**Fail**

With risk comes the possibility of failure. The greater the risk, the greater the reward, but also the greater the fall. The only way to risk is to realize you could fail. The whole point of stepping out in faith is the possibility it could all go wrong and you could blow it. The question is, how much are you willing to risk, to put on the table? That is the question most cannot fully answer. Are you willing to risk it all or just some? Are you willing to start all over again?

## To have faith you must be willing to:

**Lose:**

Mountain-moving faith comes when you are willing to lose your reputation. What people think about you and how you have built your life. Those who have radical, mountain-moving faith are those who do not seem to care what people think or say about them. One of the greatest enemies to faith is the fear of man. The fear that someone may not like you, may not agree with you, might leave you, or might talk about you is debilitating. It can destroy what God has started in you.

> **Too many times, we lack the faith to move mountains because we choose to use our position as a shovel to chip away at the mountain instead of using it to speak to the mountain.**

Mountain-moving faith comes when you are willing to lose your position. Jesus was willing to lay down His position to bring about salvation. The Bible says, "He did not consider His equality with God something to cling to" (Philippians 2:6). In other words, He was willing to lose His position in order to follow His Father.

Mountain-moving faith comes when you are willing to lose your possessions. There was a man who came to Jesus and asked what it took to be saved. He was well known and very influential. He had authority and position as well as money. Jesus told him to keep the commandments. The young man affirmed he had done just that. Jesus responded by defining what mountain-moving faith is all about. Jesus told the young man to sell all he had, give it to the poor, and follow Him. In other words, give up your position, reputation, influence, and wealth and risk it all for Christ. The young man couldn't do it. He was convinced his position was enough to move his mountains and achieve salvation.

Sometimes you have to take a leap of faith first, waiting for the trust part to come later. When Jesus laid down His position, lost His reputation, let go of His resources, He was elevated to the highest position. God has given you mountain-moving faith and wants to elevate you to the highest places. Yet this only comes when you are willing to risk it all, not part, for Him.

# Royal Favor

"FOR THE LORD GOD IS A SUN AND SHIELD; THE LORD BESTOWS FAVOR AND HONOR; NO GOOD THING DOES HE WITHHOLD FROM THOSE WHOSE WALK IS BLAMELESS." PSALM 84:11

"You know, God will give favor to anyone who will believe Him. Every day you should confess that you have favor everywhere you go. God will begin to open doors that you wouldn't believe." —Joyce Meyer, Joyce Meyer Ministries

## I Have Favor From the King of Kings

Favor is preference. When the Bible says we have favor, that means we have preference over something else. In other words, when we proclaim our dependence on God, when we walk in His way, He prefers us. He bestows favor. Things begin to happen in supernatural ways. Every area of your life can have favor: divine, supernatural preference.

When you proclaim favor from the King of kings, He will pour out favor on your family, finances and friendships. Each week at our church, we bless our people at the end of the message. The blessing is always the same:

"I bless you in your family, finances, and friendships. May you be blessed in your marriage and may your home be a lighthouse in the neighborhood. I bless you in your finances as you are faithful with what He has given you. May you have more than enough to pay your bills on time, and be faithful to give as God commands. I bless you in your relationships and friendships. That you will be the head and not the tail, the leader and not the follower. That you will be an influence in this world and not be influenced by it. I bless you today, now go and be a blessing to all those around you."

## Favor of Blessing

We believe that each person will be blessed and favored in their family, finances, and friendships. I am convinced God wants to favor and bless you.

### Family

There is supernatural favor for your marriage. Your marriage is a gift and a picture to this world. Your marriage is a picture of how God loves the church. When He pours out favor on our family, we will be a lighthouse in our neighborhoods. Your home can be a light of favor.

There is supernatural favor for your children. Your children will be blessed. Favor from the King of kings opens doors for your kids to walk through. As you raise your children, you will receive divine instruction, creative ways to discipline and guide. Your children will walk through the halls of their schools, at their jobs, with their friends all with favor (preference) on and in them.

**Finances**

There is supernatural favor for your finances. As you are faithful in what He has given you, He will supernaturally prosper you. I am always amazed at the level of immaturity in those who want to argue about giving their money to God.

Each week, we give the opportunity for people to give their tithe (10 percent of their income) and offerings in our church. We do it unapologetically. On many occasions, I have people ask me to bless them or pray for them in their finances. I simply ask if they are being faithful to give a portion of what they make back to God through the church. If they answer no, I will pray for them to receive the revelation of generosity through giving.

When I read scripture and see the level of priority God puts on giving our income back to Him through the church, and hear the debate and argument, it reminds me of when my children were very young. I would teach my children to say thank you when someone did something nice for them. It was a simple act of gratitude. Now that my children are older, this comes naturally.

Struggling with generosity in your finances is rookie-level living. If you are still arguing, debating, or conflicted about giving your money to God through the church, I challenge your level of maturity as a child of God. Get over it, grow up, write the check, give it online, rejoice, be cheerful, and let God put supernatural favor on the resources that are already His to begin with.

**Friendships**

There is supernatural favor for your friendships and relationships. You are a light, influence, and force in this world. God has placed you where you work, live, shop, play, and attend church for a purpose. That purpose is to build relationships that will influence and guide people to Him. Every day you wake up, God gives you the opportunity to be that light and influence to those around you.

## Favor of Provision

A few years ago, we had a flood in our city. Our entire neighborhood was flooded. We were boated out of our house by the National Guard. Our basement filled with water, and we were out of our home for eight weeks. During that time, we had the opportunity to put a relief tent in our front yard, and for several weeks fed the entire neighborhood breakfast, lunch, and dinner as the neighborhood was rebuilt. Many people were distraught and hopeless. We were able to pray and give hope to many families. The light of Jesus shone so bright in our neighborhood during the devastation.

> **When you proclaim you have favor, it is not for your disposal, but for others' resource.**

Just before the flood, we realized our home was in need of much repair. We made a list of what we needed to replace. The list was long and the money was short. One year after the flood, we looked at the list and realized everything we wrote down was replaced and more. More than double what we asked for was given. People could not believe how fast we were able to get help. Within a few hours of the flood receding, we had the cleanup crews show up. Several days later, electricians and carpenters were showing up. The insurance company told us to come by the office and handed us a check.

The Bible says, "...no good thing will He hold back (Psalm 84:11)." When you are favored by God, the best of the best comes, the choicest of all arrives, and you will be known as someone who walks in favor. People will comment that you seem to always come out better than before even when bad things happen. My neighbors and friends asked how we received relief and assistance so fast when others were on a waiting list. They would comment that it almost seemed like we had preferential treatment.

I decided to walk in favor and not in frustration. I didn't curse the flood but accepted it. On New Year's Eve, just three months later, we sat in that same basement (now completely finished) with family and friends and celebrated new beginnings and His favor.

> **God took care of our needs so we could take care of the needs of our neighbors.**

## Favor of Promotion

Favor means you are in line for promotion. Only God promotes. No one on earth has the authority to promote or exalt another (Psalm 75:5-7). You may get a promotion at work, or rise to the top in your field, but remember that is from God. The Bible states that as you walk through life and truly believe the King of kings has favor for you, He will exalt you. Each morning, as you lift up your praise and proclamation to Him, He hears and answers with promotion. Understand that the key to the favor is walking blameless. This is not the kind of blessing that anyone who lives gets. This is favor from the King of kings to the ones who humble themselves, walk in righteousness, and live according to His way.

Favor means you are at the top, not the bottom. You are on the summit, the heights. I love the Scripture that states He has placed us in the cleft of the rock, a high place (Psalm 27:5). It is above the storm. When difficulty comes and storms rage in your life, realize God has favored you and you rise above the storms. One of the pastors on my team shared with me an experience of being above the storm. A group of young men from The Gate (the church I lead) went on a backpacking trip around Mount McKinley in North Carolina. As they were tracking up the mountain, they stopped to look over the bluff. They didn't realize it, but they had climbed above the cloud line. When they looked out over the mountain range, all they could see below were the clouds. What was interesting was that they could see lightning in the clouds below. They were above the storm. They didn't even realize there was a storm headed their way because they had climbed above it.

When God puts favor on you, He promotes you above the storms of life. Even if you are in the middle of the storm, speak like you are above it. It may feel like you are going to be swept away, but you are not. Declare today that you are highly favored and let God lift you up and place you on the summit of the mountain. Do not fall into the squabbles, fights, and distractions of the day. You are above that, for you are highly favored. Walk like you are favored, talk like you are favored, think like you are favored because you are.

## Divine Acceptance

When you proclaim favor from the King of kings, you proclaim

His acceptance. When someone favors you, that means they accept you for who you are. Always remember, God has accepted you. He is your Father and you are His child. He states, if earthly fathers know how to bless and show favor (give good gifts) how *much more* does your Heavenly Father know how to bless and show favor? (Matthew 7:11)

Do not go through life thinking you are rejected. The spirit of rejection is a dangerous thing to connect with. You may have had many people turn their backs on you. You may have been turned down for promotions, or simply feel like life is passing you by and no one notices you. Do not let the enemy make you feel you are all alone and rejected. Every time you proclaim you have favor from the King of kings, you are proclaiming you are accepted.

Favor from God shows the world you are accepted. Your life becomes a testimony to the fact that the King of kings accepts you and promotes you. He places a special anointing on you that causes you to stand out among others.

You are able to point to Christ as one who continually blesses and keeps you. You have the opportunity to walk in acceptance and give God all the praise. The Bible is clear concerning the purpose of favor. Divine acceptance is a sign to all around. You become a testimony of the blessings and favor of God.

## Divine Favor

The favor you have is not earthly favor. It is not favor that is derived from human techniques, philosophies, or systems. This favor is not something that comes because you followed a formula and it is a scientific outcome. This favor is divine, it is favor from the King of kings:

For at the right time Christ will be revealed from heaven by the blessed and only almighty God, the King of kings and Lord of lords (1Timothy 6:15).

The favor you receive is from the highest of kings, the highest of lords. This kind of favor is not of this world, it is divine. Realize that when you are favored, the King of kings and Lord of lords rejoices over you. He deals well with you and is good to you. You have made Him glad and He wants and does right by you.

God will use any means to pour favor on His children. Sometimes divine favor comes through the very obstacle that is keeping you from the favor of God. When the children of Israel were still slaves in Egypt, the Lord spoke to Moses to tell the people to ask the Egyptians for their gold and silver. In Exodus 3, God said He would cause the Egyptians to look favorably on the Israelites. The Israelites were slaves and the Egyptians were the masters. Yet favor from the King of kings can come through the master and bring promotion and provision to the slave. You see, the favor the Egyptians showed the Israelites was not from the Egyptians but from God. You may feel like you are bound, burdened, or even buried by life. Just remember, you have favor from the King of kings, and His favor just might come through the very thing that is binding, burdening, or burying you.

Favor from the King of kings and Lord of lords is high praise from heaven. This is not something to become arrogant and boastful about because within favor is benevolence. It is the realization that we cannot do it on our own and we must have favor from someone who has access to greater resources than we do. Divine favor is simply someone helping carry the load, showing consideration and mercy, lifting the burden for those who cannot do it all by themselves. When we were favored by God during the flood, we were able to favor others. Allow the favor of God to flow through you to those around you.

# Cosmic Future

> "SO DON'T BE SO SURPRISED WHEN I TELL YOU THAT YOU HAVE TO BE 'BORN FROM ABOVE'—OUT OF THIS WORLD, SO TO SPEAK."
> JOHN 3:7 (MSG)

"We are made wise not by the recollection of our past, but by the responsibility for our future." —George Bernard Shaw

"The best way to predict the future is to create it" —Abraham Lincoln

## A Future that is out of this World

When I was in third grade, I had a terrible time understanding math and reading. My grades were awful, and I was not able to keep up with the other kids. As a result, I was held back and put into second grade. When the decision was made for me to go back to second grade, my mom asked if I wanted to go to another school where none of the kids knew me. She told me it might be easier than facing all my friends. I decided to stay in the school where I was. I will never forget that first day back. I stood in the second-grade line as all my third-grade friends kept yelling at me to get in line with them. They didn't know I had been put back. That was a tough day.

I remember being asked why I didn't want to go to a different school, where I could simply walk in as a new second grader. I told them that if I could not face that today, I knew there would be things in my future I would not have the strength to face. There have been so many mountains and valleys, trials and triumphs, wins and losses, defeats and victories since that day in second grade, part two. Some I have faced with courage and strength, and some I have faced with fear and doubt. But that day on the playground, facing my second chance, was a defining moment. I knew I was being molded for the incredible future ahead of me. I knew this difficult situation would mold me into someone who could face failure, rejection, and victory.

God loves you so much, He has a future for you that is not of this world. It is a future that will not harm you or tear you down (Jeremiah 29:11). It is a future that will put you on the top, not the bottom. Eugene H. Peterson, in the Message version of the Bible, says He will make you the top dog and not the bottom dog (Deuteronomy 28:13). We are meant to be rulers and kings; that is our future. Remember, you are in this world, but you are not of this world. You are in a new kingdom. You are a new creation (2 Corinthians 5:17). Your future is amazing. Jesus has gone away to prepare a place for you. (John 14). Stop and read Revelation 21 to discover the place being prepared for you. It is absolutely beyond imagination. When you fix your thoughts on your future and you proclaim that future every day, you will be encouraged and know that nothing can defeat you. Nothing can harm you.

## Past Future

Too many times, our future is dictated by the circumstances of today or the events of the past. A broken marriage, a failed business, abusive or absent parents, a job loss, death, or sickness, all can be the guiding force that dictates our future. We allow our present circumstances to name our future.

A 2018 Deloitte survey noted the outlook of the next generation concerning the future is not that positive.[1] Only 8 percent of millennials believe they will be financially better off than their parents. The outlook for the coming leaders of our communities, states, churches, and nation is very pessimistic about the society we live in and the future of the society they will lead.

This is in direct conflict with what the Word of God says. Our future is out of this world. While there may be good reason to be skeptical of the future in our society, as a child of God, you can look the future in the eye and proclaim that your future is bright.

## Present Future

There is a story in the Bible of a young woman who was pregnant. She was the daughter-in law-of the leader of the nation of Israel. In one day, her husband and father-in-law died because Israel was at war. During that same battle, a very important chest was taken by the enemy army. This chest represented the presence of God. It was called the Arc of the Covenant. When that chest was in the right place, it meant God was in the right place, He was guiding everything through His leaders. When Eli and Phenaes (Eli's son, the woman's husband) died and the chest of God was stolen, it was truly a dark day.

The pressure on the young woman was so great that she immediately went into labor. At the moment she was about to die, she gave birth to a son and named him Ichabod, which means "the Glory of the Lord has departed." She was so devastated by the events of that one day. She was at death's door. She couldn't see past the present, and before she died, named her son God Left.

Your name is your identity. It describes you. Think of someone with whom you had difficulty or didn't like in the past. How do you feel about that name? When you were deciding what to name your son or daughter and someone mentioned a name they liked, you said, "No way; I knew a girl with that name..." or, "Yeah, I had a teacher with that name who really made a difference in my life. I really like that name."

Names have meaning. This young woman identified her and her son's future with that name. She could have named him God Is Coming Back, or God Is Still God. She could have named him The Glory of the Lord Is Returning, or The Lord Will Always Be with Us. She, instead, chose to name her son's future, The Glory of the Lord Departed. Every time he walked into the room, everyone was reminded that God had left. Every time he saw his name, or one of his friends called for him, they were reminded that God had left. God had *NOT* left. But it is so difficult to continue in faith when your very identity, your name, describes your present and defines your future.

## Personal Future

Do not name your future based on your present. Do not do what

Ichabod's mother did. Realize that what you are going through at this moment or what has happened to you in the past has no bearing on what God has for you in the future. You may feel like all hope is gone, there is no way out, and you are crumbling under the pressure of life. But always remember that God has already made a way of escape for you (1 Corinthians 10:13).

At times, you will be tempted to quit, throw in the towel, give up, or curse the situation you are in. Do not do it. You may feel that you are being held back or pulled back, but realize you are being pulled back only to be thrust out farther than you ever thought possible, like an arrow in an archer's bow.

The key is to trust that God has an incredible future with your name on it. I have heard many people say that God will never give you more than you can handle. That simply is not true. There will be times when life is so difficult, so overwhelming, so devastating that without Christ, you will buckle under the pressure. Keep in mind, with every situation, there is already a path for you to walk through (Isaiah 43:19). Keep your eyes focused on the future.

You may not always like the situation in which you find yourself. You may not like the things God allows in your life or His ways of doing things. In fact, you may flat-out disagree with some of His decrees. But there is one thing for certain: God has an incredible future in store for you. It is out of this world, and that will never change. Do not curse your future simply because you do not understand the present. Do not name your future according to the circumstances you see. They may seem dark and you may be walking through the valley of death and death's shadow is enveloping you. You may be in a state of confusion and convinced this is your place in life. That is only what the enemy wants you to see. My question for you is, What are you look at?

What you say and see today can and will determine your tomorrow. How are you planning, strategizing, and envisioning? What is your life going to look like in one, five, ten, or twenty years? Several years ago, I started a routine in my life. I map out my life goals and what I want to accomplish. I write them down and display them so I do not forget them. In my office, I have a vision wall, a map of the next thirty years and what I believe God wants to do in our church and community. When I get discouraged, I look up and see the vision wall. Some days, it is a bit daunting; other days, it is inspiring. One thing is for sure: The picture of my future, on that wall, reminds me I am here for a purpose greater than myself. Every time I walk into my office, I realize the decisions we are making today will affect next year, next decade, and the next generation.

God has placed in you an incredible vision, an incredible future. Do not name what is in you Ichabod simply because of what you are going through right now. God has not left you. His glory has not departed from you. He has anointed you, blessed you, promised to never leave you. No matter if it feels like the enemy has stolen the very presence of God from you and placed Him in a foreign camp. Know this: He is causing the enemy to fall at His feet. The enemy may try to attack you and convince you that you are confused, cursed, and condemned, but know this: You are confident, courageous, and victorious. Your future is bright.

# Notes

1. Deloitte Millennial Survey https://www2.deloitte.com/content/dam/Deloitte/global/Documents/About-Deloitte/gx-2018-millennial-survey-report.pdf

# Ancient Foundation

"ALL SCRIPTURE IS INSPIRED BY GOD AND IS USEFUL TO TEACH US WHAT IS TRUE AND TO MAKE US REALIZE WHAT IS WRONG IN OUR LIVES. IT CORRECTS US WHEN WE ARE WRONG AND TEACHES US TO DO WHAT IS RIGHT." 2 TIMOTHY 3:16

"Every institution in which men are not increasingly occupied with the Word of God must become corrupt."
—Martin Luther

## My Foundation Is the Word of God

The Word of God is transcendent, which means to go beyond the usual limits of ordinary experience, time, or culture. Throughout life, culture, governmental structures, race, education, money, and time, the Word of God is the transcendent foundation of all mankind. When I was a boy, we sang a little song, "The B-I-B-L-E, yes that's the book for me. I stand upon the Word of God. The B-I-B-L-E." The truth was ingrained into us that the Bible is good for every event, situation, valley, or victory we face.

Foundations in life are important. The strength of any building, institution, or country is dependent on its foundation. If you are going to be strong in life, you need a strong and secure foundation. Once you proclaim you are a child of God, you have a new foundation. A foundation that does not change. If the foundation continues to change or shift, you will never be stable. Your life's foundation cannot be something that shifts or changes depending on the season or culture. The Bible says a doubting man is unstable in all his ways (James 1:8).

Foundations set the size and scope of the building. Whatever your foundation is will determine the size and scope of your life. Jesus is called the chief cornerstone because He sets the size and scope of our life. He is also called the Word. He is our foundation and the Word of God is the written and "now" Word we stand on. The Word does not change nor can it be edited. We should not add to or subtract from the Word. Believers accept all of it as the inspired word, good for correction, instruction, and life boundaries.

The foundation of a building is unseen. It is the part of the building that is underground and deep. The Word of God must go deep in our lives. It is not something you continue to wave around like a badge, a banner, or a placard. I am not saying that we hide our beliefs or Godly concepts. But the foundation of the building is not what is seen. The foundation is what makes the building able to withstand the high winds of a storm. The foundation is what keeps the walls of the building from crumbling. It is what keeps those inside the building safe. If the foundation is not deep, solid, and sure, those who live in the building are not safe.

The same goes for your marriage, family, relationships, finances, and career—your whole life. Without a solid, sure, deep foundation, you cannot build a safe, secure home. Each day we proclaim our foundation is the Word of God. We are told that everything on this earth is going to pass away. Heaven, earth...everything is going to pass away. But His Word will never pass away. The Word of God is transcendent through all cultures, ages, laws, kingdoms, and governments. There is no law that can supersede the Word of God. It is the very foundation of life and everything is built on it.

The Word of God is not archaic, outdated, or obsolete. It can be used in every area of life. The Apostle Paul understood the importance and use of the Bible. He wrote to his young apostle/apprentice Timothy that the Word of God is inspired and profitable (2 Timothy 3:16). The Word can be used to reprove, correct, train, and equip. Paul points out in his letter to Timothy that each of these areas set a framework for you to establish the Bible as your transcendent, solid foundation.

## Inspired

The Bible is our foundation because it is from God. The Word is inspired by God. Each writer was directed by the Spirit to be the writer, and the Spirit is the Author. The inspiration for the ideas, concepts, theologies, philosophies, and strategies did not come from the minds of men or the underpinnings of the social context. They came from the very mind and heart of God, who is the Author. The Spirit inspired,

> **The concepts and philosophies found in the Bible are the thoughts, creed, and story of the Creator of the universe.**

downloaded, and guided each writer to impart these transcendent concepts to the page so we might have a sure life plan to follow.

## Profitable

When the Word of God is your foundation, you have an advantage in your teaching. The Bible is from the one who knows how the systems of the world work. Family systems, governmental systems, legal systems, economic systems, and cultural systems all function better when they are understood from a biblical foundation and perspective. As a child of God, who has the foundation of the Word of God, you start every day with an advantage over those who do not proclaim the Word of God as their foundation. There is great profit in establishing your life on the Word of God.

## Test

Every time there is a historical discovery, a scientific breakthrough, or an archaeological find, it proves the Bible is correct. Stories of men who have sought to disprove the Bible have ended their search in complete and total faith in the words of these books. You can test any theory, concept, or thought you may have to the foundational teaching of the Bible, and you will discover whether the theory, concept, or thought will be successful.

This is the difficult part of the Word of God. It points out our failures or convicts us of our wrongdoing. This is the place where many will ignore or simply cut out the part of the Word of God that offends or contradicts their lifestyle or belief. The act of ignoring certain teachings and standards of the Bible in order to bypass the reality that you are not living according to the ways and mandates of a child of God is quite extensive. Entire theologies and doctrines have been based on the belief that certain parts of the Bible are no longer in force.

Some say those teachings were for another day. However, if the entire, meaning all, total, leave-nothing-out Word of God is for reproof, then we cannot simply eliminate what we don't understand, like, or makes us uncomfortable. Either the Word of God is our foundation or it is not. You cannot decide which part of the foundation of your house you are going to pay attention to and which part you are going to ignore or do away with. That would be foolish. For your house to stand, you need the whole foundation. In the same way, for your life to function in every area fully, you need the entire foundation, the entire Word of God.

## Correction

The Bible is the instrument for course correction. The Word of God straightens the crooked paths, turns question marks into exclamation points, and uprights the bent.

> **The Bible is the measuring rod for life. It is the plumb line of the architect and the compass to the wanderer.**

There is very little margin for error in life. That is why we are encouraged to keep the Word of God as our foundation. A simple miscalculation of less than a degree in the trajectory of an airplane can cause the plane to be miles off course; 80 percent of the instruments in the cockpit of an airplane are designed to keep it on course. By the very nature of gravity, wind and resistance left without the instruments of correction, the plane would not ever be on course or arrive at its prescribed destination.

In the same way, the Bible tells us we are all born with a bend away from where God wants us to be. Without course correction instruments in our life, we will constantly be crashing to the ground, go off course, or head in the opposite direction of our target.

There is a tendency to redefine what the Bible says or explain it away as written for a different time or society. Realize you cannot change the Word of God to fit your lifestyle. That is like Charlie Brown in the *Peanuts* cartoon shooting the arrow and then drawing the target around the arrow. You might feel like you are succeeding at life and hitting the target, but what good is hitting a target you define if it is not the same target God has defined? The Bible says there is a way that seems right to us, but in the end leads to failure, destruction, and even death (Proverbs 14:12). Left to your own ways of doing things, you will raise your children, love your spouse, build your career, spend your money, and all the while think it is right, but quite probably, you are heading for failure.

Yet with the Word of God as your foundation, you will be the one who, in the face of resistance, storms, headwinds, or complete darkness, lead your family through to incredible victories, mountaintop experiences, and favor from your Father who is in Heaven!!!

## Training

The Word of God is a partner, a coach in a sense that comes alongside you and trains you for life. It is the best companion for training children, coaching teenagers, and mentoring young adults through the decisions of marriage, career, parenting, and self-improvement. The Word of God is not a reference guide you occasionally consult, or a resource to add to your collection of resources. It is THE source for all things life!!! If the Word of God is not the foundation of your life and the transcendent standard by which you measure everything, you will go off course. And as Martin Luther stated, "Every institution in which men are not increasingly occupied with the Word of God must become corrupt."

There is nothing you can face in raising and training your children for which the Word of God does not give instruction. It is the whole training and education in areas of morals, mind-sets, convictions, physical fitness, finances, relationships, and matters of life and death. The Word of God is all-inclusive in instructing and training.

Training can also mean how you guide something to grow in a certain direction. It is the idea behind "Train a child in the way they should go and when they become old they will go that way" (Prov. 22:6). Several years ago, our team started a housing development organization. During one of our projects several trees were planted in the development. As the landscaper was putting in the young trees, he would tie them off and stake them into the ground. He later told me that he always trains the young trees early so they will grow straight and tall. He said that if he did not do it, something could happen when he wasn't around that would cause them to grow crooked or at an angle.

It is your responsibility as a parent to train those in your family to live a certain way. In the same way as a garden grows and needs to be weeded, your life and your family's lives need training only to allow certain things to grow, and grow in a trained way. If you allow the garden to grow without any attention, it will revert back to its original state.

The way the Word of God becomes a trainer and coach is by studying it. Devouring every part of it. As believers, we are to work diligently to be able to correctly explain the Word of God. It does not make much sense to proclaim your foundation is the Word of God every day if you are not able to correctly explain and apply it. Being a confident child of God, someone who is not ashamed of their work, requires understanding and the ability to correctly explain the Word of God.

## Equipped

My father-in-law had every tool you could imagine in his garage. If there was a project I was working on, something in the house that needed to be fixed, or the mower wouldn't start, my father-in-law had a tool to finish the job, fix the problem, or start the engine. No matter what, you could count on him to have the tool to start and complete the job.

When the Word of God is your foundation, you have the tools to tackle the jobs of life. The Word of God, as your foundation, perfectly furnishes you with everything you need for a believer's lifestyle. There is not one tool, understanding, knowledge, concept, or philosophy that cannot be found in the Word of God to complete the task God has called you to accomplish. Without the Word of God, it is like trying to build a house with cake decorating tools, or fix a car with a draftsman's compass and an accountant's calculator. The jobs and the tools do not match. In the same way, you need the tools that are perfectly matched for building a life. The list of tools are found in the Word of God, and once you have acquired these tools, the Word of God is the instruction manual that will guide you in how to use them.

The Word says you will be equipped for every good work. When you proclaim every day that your foundation is the Word of God, you are proclaiming that you are setting out to do good works and that you are equipped, perfectly furnished, and trained to deal with whatever comes along. No matter if what comes is a storm, a valley, a trial, death, destruction, victory, a mountaintop experience, poverty, or prosperity, you will be ready to turn it into a good work for your family, friends, community, and church.

You are equipped through the Word of God to be a good father, mother, spouse, employee, employer, financial consultant, entrepreneur, champion, victor, warrior, and conqueror. Proclaim it every day: My foundation is the Word of God.

The word of God is the source for all things in life, and every day we proclaim—our foundation is the Word of God!!!

# Surefooted

> "HE MAKES ME AS SUREFOOTED AS A DEER, ENABLING ME TO STAND ON MOUNTAIN HEIGHTS." PSALM 18:33

When you walk alone, when everybody is against you, if you are sure with your ideas, walk strongly and proudly as if there is an army of angels by your side!" —Mehmet Murat Ildan, Turkish Playwrit

## My Walk is Sure

Remember the old Bee Gees song, "Stayin' Alive"? The first line of the song states you can tell what a person is up to by the way they walk. Well, I'm not sure the point of our walk is to convey what the song implies, but you can tell by the way someone walks through life how sure they are of who they are and where they are going. Even in a physical sense, I have known immediately when someone walked into a room how sure they are about themselves and where they are in life. Our walk is crucial to our belief.

If we are not sure about where we are going, we will not be sure of the steps we are to take. To be sure in our walk, we must know where we want to end up. There is a scene in the 1951 Disney production of *Alice's Adventures in Wonderland*, when Alice falls into the rabbit hole and finds herself in Wonderland. She does not know where she is, what to do, or where to go. As she stands there pondering her predicament, the Cheshire Cat appears on a signpost. The signpost had many arrows pointing in all different directions. Alice looks up and asks the Cheshire Cat, "Which way do I go?" He retorts, "Where do you want to end up?" To that, Alice responds, "I don't know." "Well then," the Cheshire Cat replies, "it doesn't matter which way you go."

Believers know which way to walk because they know where they want to end up. Therefore, a child of God can say with all confidence, "My walk is sure!" You may feel like you have passed into an unknown land, or have no idea how to get out of the situation you are in. Always remember, you know where you are going no matter where you are right now. The sure walk of the believer is a walk of humility, protection, purpose, and prosperity.

## Humble walk

I am amazed at how easy it is to become prideful and arrogant. It is the cause of Satan's great fall from heaven, a leader's fall from grace, and God-given visions and dreams being thwarted before they are completed. There have been many times when true men and women of God begin to walk in their anointing and fall into great temptation to become prideful and take credit.

Do not fall into the trap of thinking your sure walk is due to your own knowledge and wisdom. When you proclaim, *your walk is sure*, make sure it is not a proclamation of conceit and arrogance but rather a proclamation of humility and reliance. It doesn't matter where you walk, or what the circumstances are, God is with you. His Word says, even if you go through the flood, fire, valley of death, or persecution, do not fear, your Father in heaven is with you. Jesus's last words to you, "I will be with you to the end..." (Matthew 28:19, 20) is how you have a sure walk. Your walk is not in *your* power, strength, or knowledge but in *His* presence and Spirit.

Each one of us, as a child of God, has been given a measure of grace and faith, but that does not give us the right to be prideful. Paul, in Romans 12, tells us we are not to think too highly of ourselves, but to always judge ourselves with common sense and self-control. In other words, do not become arrogant and blind simply because you are confident in what God has called you to do and where He has called you to go.

**Protected walk**

Several years ago, we moved into a new home, in a new community. There was a lot of sickness in our family and we didn't know what had been going on in the home prior to us moving in. One morning, Vicki was praying and heard the spirit of God say to her, "Get up and prayer walk around your house seven times." She first thought, *I can't do that; what will the neighbors think?"* Yet she obeyed. To this day, we have marked that moment in time when Vicki marched and prayed around our home seven times as the mark of miracles.

There is a story in the Bible about a very sick captain in a distant land. His name was Naaman. He had led many campaigns against Israel and taken many captives. Naaman was a valued leader for his king, but he was also struck with leprosy. One day, Naaman's servant, an Israelite girl, mentioned he should go see the prophet in Israel and be healed. So Naaman set out for Israel and met with the Israelite king to see if he could be healed. Word reached Elisha, the prophet in the area. Elisha called for Naaman. Naaman went to see him, but when Elisha heard Naaman was outside the door, Elisha sent his servant with instructions. The instructions for healing were simple: go down and dip into the Jordan River seven times and he would be healed. This infuriated Naaman. He felt he could have stayed home and dipped into any of the rivers in his land. Naaman set off for his home, although his servants pleaded with him. They reasoned that if the prophet had given Naaman something difficult to do, he would have accepted the challenge. Yet something so simple and seemingly beneath his rank was an offense.

Sometimes, God asks us to do the simple to receive the miracle. Naaman listened and went to the Jordan River. He dipped once, twice, and finally the seventh time. When he came out of the water on the seventh dip, the Bible states his skin "was as healthy as the skin of a young child" (2 Kings 5). Don't despise the way God chooses for you to walk. Don't despise the way God chooses for you to step out.

Since my wife's prayer walk, the list of healings and miracles over the past sixteen years in our home have been amazing. My youngest was instantly healed of asthma. A lump in Vicki's breast simply dissolved between the doctor's waiting room and the exam room. During the same time, Vicki was diagnosed with some additional health issues. We again claimed healing and miracles. We went to our trusted doctor to ask what needed to be done, and he ran tests to confirm the diagnosis. When the tests came back, our doctor said there was no disease of any kind in her blood. She was completely healthy, with no sickness of any kind. We now had taken two tests, one saying there was disease, the other saying her walk was sure. We have had financial miracle after miracle after miracle. When God calls you to walk, walk sure. Do not be intimidated, fearful, or ashamed of where God is calling you to walk. Stand strong and walk sure.

## Purposed walk

Everywhere your foot lands, that is your ground. God told Abraham, "This is your land, walk on it." Believers walk with purpose; they walk with a plan. Where are you walking today? Remember, everywhere you walk is claimed for God. Your home, your neighborhood, your school, your work, your church, your community.

On March 1, 1989, my wife and I began pastoring. When we first arrived in the area, my assignment was student ministries. I loved being a youth pastor. To this day, there will be times I miss the excitement and adventure of that student ministry. Within three weeks of our being at the church, I received a call from the city, asking if our youth group could help clean up a fifty-acre abandoned residential development that was previously a train yard. I agreed, knowing all I had to do was get a grill and some hot dogs and turn a community cleanup project into a youth party. No brainer.

I went to scope out the land. What I didn't realize was, the vacant land was right behind our church property. For the next several hours, I walked on that land. I found abandoned streets, abandoned cars, tires, shopping carts and makeshift shelters for those without homes. As I walked, I sensed the Lord speaking to me. Then He started showing me a vision of homes, buildings, parks, and ponds. In the vision, I realized God wanted to take what was abandoned and turn it into a thriving community.

In the vision, I saw unwed mothers' homes, missionary housing, apartments for transitional housing, units for couples having difficulty in their marriages, shelter for abused women, dorms for college students. I quickly went to pick up my wife and brought her back to the land. We stood in the middle of the property and I began to point out all the different things God had showed me. I knew this was my purpose. Something lit up in me, and I couldn't put it out if I wanted to.

Joshua was the second leader of the Israelite nation after they were released from Egypt. Moses had died, and now Joshua led his people into the promised land. When they came to the city of Jericho, God told Joshua to march around the city for seven days. The walls were fortified, tall, and impossible to humanly penetrate. The walls of Jericho were six feet thick and up to ninety-five feet tall. The foolishness of Joshua was laughable to the skeptic. But God told him to walk, to march around those walls, for seven days with his army.

What looks impossible for you today? Are there walls built high, giants looming large, or enemies baring down in your life? Just keep walking. Remember, the one who commanded you to walk is taller than any wall, bigger than any giant, and mightier than any army.

> **When you are facing impossible odds, God is saying keep walking, keep marching, and make some noise.**

On the seventh day of Joshua's march, God instructed him to march around the city seven times. The circumference of Jericho was approximately a half mile. Joshua and his army marched for three and a half miles on that last day. The walls of Jericho were so vast that those in the inner core inside would have had no idea that anyone was marching around the city. At the end of the seventh round, he was instructed to blow a trumpet and light torches. At that moment, the walls started to crumble. Archaeologists found that the walls fell flat and were burned.

> **When you walk the way God tells you to walk, with the purpose He has set for you, the walls come down and victory is sure!**

I started walking that abandoned land every day. Two years later, my wife and I became the Lead pastor of the church. I would go early on Sunday and walk on those abandoned streets seven times. One day, I received a call that a developer had been given the land by the city, to develop a residential community. I was not pleased at all because that was *my* land I had walked, and the Bible says wherever you place your foot is your land. I asked God why He hadn't given it to me. I distinctly heard Him ask me, "Do you know how to build a residential development?" I realized there was something very big happening. Shortly after the land transaction, the developer came to me and asked what kind of church we were. I told him, and he was of the same faith. He smiled and asked if I would be willing to trade some land with him and become partners in developing the land. Immediately, we were in partnership and ownership of the entire development.

Twenty-eight years later, at the time of the writing of this book, all the buildings, parks, homes, and green spaces I saw have now been built. We own fifteen acres of the development and are working on acquiring the rest. When God says He will give you the land your foot sets on, believe Him and walk sure and with purpose. He will provide as long as you keep walking!

## Prosperous walk

God promises that He will bless you as you walk through this life. But the blessings and prosperity come when you walk blameless and selective. Be careful who you walk with. The Bible is very clear that your confidence and sure walk have a lot to do with who you walk with. You will be blessed if you do not walk with those who are constantly trying to get you to do things that are not of God. (Psalm 1:1)

As a child of God, you are responsible for walking in the way the Lord has directed you to walk. As you continue to walk in His ways, you will prosper, live long, and possess the land He has called you to possess (Deuteronomy 5:33). It doesn't matter what is going on in your life. If the road seems too treacherous, the valley too deep, or the mountain too high, you will not lose your footing. We are told that when we walk in His ways, our steps will not be tangled, and when we run, we will not stumble (Proverbs 4:12). Realize this sure walk is flood-proof, fire-proof, death-, destruction-, and danger-proof. Does that mean you will not have floods, fires, death, destruction, and danger in your life? No! I wish I could tell you that the sure walk of the child of God is problem- and storm-free, but that simply is not true. You will have all of those things; they simply will not have the power to overtake you. Your walk is sure! You will not be overwhelmed!

# Bold Words

> "WORDS SATISFY THE MIND AS MUCH AS FRUIT DOES THE STOMACH; GOOD TALK IS AS GRATIFYING AS A GOOD HARVEST."
> PROVERBS 18:20 (MSG)

"Talking with quiet confidence will always beat screaming with obvious insecurity." —Unknown

## My Talk is Confident

"The way you talk is a high priority as a child of God," Paul states in Ephesians 4:29 (MSG), "Watch the way you talk. Let nothing foul or dirty come out of your mouth. Say only what helps, each word a gift."

The more we talk confidently, the more we are full in our spirit. Your words have power. The power to bless and the power to curse, the power to give life and the power to give death are in your words. The believer speaks with confidence because believers know what to say. King Solomon wrote, "Words satisfy the mind as much as fruit does the stomach; good talk is as gratifying as a good harvest" (Proverbs 18:20). In other words, your words feed your mind. How satisfied is your mind? Do you have trouble with your thoughts? If so, it could be because of the way you talk.

What are you saying today? Think back over the last twenty-four hours and ask yourself about your talk. What did you say to your spouse, your kids, your boss, your neighbors, or your co-workers? Did you talk blessings or curses, confidence or confusion, uplifting or tearing down? The Apostle Paul in his letter to the Ephesian believers states that every word that comes out of our mouth is a gift (Ephesians 4:29). What kind of gifts are you giving today?

Each morning, I spend time with God and ask Him to give me words for my family. I believe God wants to give us timely, and current words for those in our lives. One morning, I was sitting in my regular seat in our family room. I asked my youngest daughter, Victoria, to please get me a cup of coffee. As she was handing me the cup, a thought came into my mind: There is going to be a man who loves you as much and in the same way as I love your mom. I simply looked at Victoria and told her what I was thinking. The night before, unbeknownst to me, her boyfriend had broken up with her. She was feeling like there would never be anyone for her. At that moment, I was able to talk confidently to her about her future. Believers speak with confidence!

## Watch your talk...Watch your words

It is so easy to slip into the kind of talk that is all around us. Negative news, disrespectful language, harsh and vulgar words all are part of the mainstream culture today. It seems the cruder and harsher you speak, the more "in" you will become. This is why Paul said, "watch the way you talk..." (MSG). "Let no unwholesome word..." (NASB) In other words, we control what comes out of our mouth. Every thought does not have to be shared. Every action by those around us does not need a comment. In this day of self-promotion and aggrandizement, the temptation to give commentary on every event going on in someone else's life, to criticize and bash others in order to lift ourselves up, can be formidable. A child of God proclaims a different kind of speech.

There is a sense that the day is coming when you will need to be very conscience of every word, thought, or phrase that comes out of your mouth. Paul was very clear in how you are to speak: "...only what helps, each word a gift" (MSG). We should focus our words on lifting others up above ourselves, and to make those around us confident in who they are.

Confident talk is a gift to those who hear it. Each week, I have the opportunity to either beat down or lift up those who hear me speak. You have the same opportunity every time you walk into a room, meet with a friend, or say good morning to your spouse and children.

**Your talk is your choice. You choose to either be a giver or a taker with your words every time you speak.**

The key to every word being a gift is to pay attention. Don't let your feelings or thoughts simply run out of your mouth. I have to be very conscience of the fact that I can tend to let my mouth run without thinking. This may be a little crude, but I once heard someone say, "She has diarrhea of the mouth and constipation of the brain." Let's not be guilty of that same thing. The constant battle to watch the way we talk can be won. There are a few things we can do to make sure that every word we speak is a gift.

## 4 rules of confident talk

**1. Filter what you hear.**

Every time you open your mouth to speak, ask yourself:

- Will these words give or take?
- Do they uplift or tear down?
- Do they encourage or discourage?
- Do they challenge for change or berate?
- Check the motive of your heart to see if you truly want to lift up the person, or is there a hidden agenda, competition, or critical spirit.

**2. Always gripe up and never down**

You will lose your influence and show your insecurity if you practice griping to your peers and/or those you lead. Never do that. If you have something you need to deal with, go to those who are leaders above you. They are the ones who can do something about it.

**3. Determine that everyone around you is better than you.**

You may be the smartest person in the room, but don't talk like it. Enter every conversation or situation realizing you can learn something from anyone. The Bible tells us to treat others as better than ourselves, and that goes for our talk as well. (Philippians 2:3)

**4. Connect with a confidant**

We all need someone we can talk to, confide in, and at times vent to. This is different than griping. Have a trusted confidant to whom you can share, who may or may not be able to help or give guidance. They are simply there to let you get out what you need to. Sometimes our thoughts are not all that good, and they need to come out of our mouths to prove it. Having a trusted someone in your life you can talk to without judgment will save you from a world of hurt if you shoot off your mouth.

## Confident talk

Confidence is the by-product of true belief. Confidence is the slave to belief. In other words, you can be confident in something you truly believe but confidently wrong. Confidence does not dictate our beliefs; beliefs dictate our confidence. If you are going to be confident in your talk, you have to have a solid belief system. There are certain things you do not need belief or confidence in, in order to speak confidently. For example, when the sun comes out, you can confidently say the sun is shining right now. There is no need for belief or confidence because your words are based on fact; they are based on what you can see.

But when there is room for opinion, faith, belief, or doubt, confidence can and will escape. We seek a second opinion, look for those who agree with us, and ultimately talk without confidence or conviction. Believers will talk confidently, as if something is fact even if it hasn't happened yet.

Paul says that we are to believe in the One who speaks as if things are, even though they are not (Romans 4:17). To have confidence in the One who can speak things into existence. To speak like a believer means you are going to risk being wrong, looking foolish, or standing on an unseen foundation. This is why our walk comes before our talk. We act like we believe and our words follow. When your children do not act or speak like champions, you still call them champions.

During the time Israel was being harassed and beaten down by Midian (Judges 6), the Angel of the Lord visited Gideon, the youngest son of the youngest tribe. His walk was not sure and his talk was definitely not confident. The Angel found him cowering in a wine press threshing wheat. He was afraid of the enemy, and rightly so. He, and his nation, was no match for the enemy. They were being thwarted at every turn. Yet Gideon was a child of Abraham, Isaac, and Jacob. His birth order, physical size, intellect, and possessions made no difference to the captain of the Host. The captain didn't approach Gideon to address his fear, position, or lack of confidence. The captain came to him on the authority of the King of Kings! He called to him as "mighty warrior." Gideon was not acting or talking like a mighty warrior, but after that session in the wine press, he was not only talking and acting like a mighty warrior, he *was* a mighty warrior!

When you are confident, you will not hold back. You will not be timid in your approach or your words. This is why the writer of Hebrews said to enter into the presence of God with boldness (confidence). Joshua told his men not to hold back, not to be timid but to be confident. Joshua defeated five kings with the nation of Israel. When they captured the kings, he brought them in front of the entire Israelite army. Joshua called for the five field generals to come forward. Each general placed his boot on the neck of the kings. Then Joshua said, "This is what happens to your enemy when you trust in Him." God is looking for His children to proclaim with confidence, not to hold back but to put their boot on the neck of the enemy.

Gideon left that wine press never to return to his fear, hiding, and low self-esteem. He became a mighty warrior, just as the captain of the Host said he would. Our talk becomes aligned with whoever we believe in.

Victoria eventually married the young man who broke up with her that night. They had a dream wedding and all seemed to be good. I didn't know at the time I spoke those words the difficulty we as a family were going to face. About a year and a half after they were married, we found out there was physical and emotional abuse in their home from the beginning of their marriage. But I had spoken those words to her: "There is a man who will love you as much and the same way I love your mom." Victoria held on to that promise but eventually, because of the continued abuse, separated from her husband while seeking reconciliation.

Things seemed to be getting better and we were hopeful that this man was going to be the one I felt God had showed me that morning years before. But on May 2, 2015, he disappeared. For forty-one days, we searched and searched. Neighbors, friends, family, and even people we did not know helped in the search. After those agonizing days, we received a call. An unobserved accident had occurred and his car was found at the bottom of a retention pond in a local neighborhood. Tragically, our worst fears were realized. Her husband was in the car, and Victoria, at the age of twenty-three, was a widow with twin girls.

What do you do about that? I began to doubt. Had I missed what God was saying? Did I misinterpret the divine message? This was a very dark time for our family. We held on to one another, as God held on to us. We could feel His presence in every moment. Yet what about the confident word I had received as a reassurance for my daughter? In my heart, I knew I had heard Him speak. So I continued to hold on to that promise for my daughter.

Time passed, and Victoria began to heal. Eventually she felt very strongly that God had someone for her. Within a few months, another young man came into her life, and they married. One day Victoria was talking to Vicki, and in passing said, "Mom, I am so happy. This is what I always saw for my life." When I heard those words, God gently reminded me of the confident words I had spoken to my daughter several years before.

I do not assume to understand why children of God go through difficult times of death and darkness. I wish I could explain to you the depths of God's heart in all the mountains and valleys He allows us to experience, but I cannot. I do know this one thing—when He gives you a word, hold on to it. Speak it loud and strong. Declare it. Proclaim it. And always remember, your talk is confident.

# Divine Attitude

## "YOUR ATTITUDE SHOULD BE THE SAME THAT CHRIST JESUS HAD." PHILIPPIANS 2:5

"People may hear your words, but they feel your attitude." —John C. Maxwell

## My Attitude Is Like Christ's

To have the attitude of Christ means to side with Him, or to be of His party. We are living in a time in which your attitude will be the same as the one you side with. To have the attitude of Christ is to understand how He thinks, speaks, acts, and walks. When you proclaim that your attitude aligns with Christ's, you align your focus, view, and perspective to that which Christ focuses on, what His view is, and what His perspective is. Understand that this kind of attitude means you are so aligned with the way Christ thinks that it is almost impossible to tell the difference between your way of thinking and Christ's.

We are expected to have the attitude of Christ. The Apostle Paul was not merely suggesting or recommending that we have it.

No, he said, "Have this attitude…" This is not something that is an option for the Christ-follower, a child of God. This is the expectation, the norm for the believer, not the exception.

Your attitude is so important because your attitude is reflected in your behavior. You can see on your face, the light in your eye, the posture in which you stand, and the way you walk what your attitude is. Your attitude will be the first thing that enters the room, emanates from your presence, and stays long after you leave.

Your attitude will affect how you see, process, and filter things. Your attitude will determine the level of excellence you put into your work, family, relationships, self, and community. When your attitude is bad, pretty much everything you do, say, touch, or have around reflects the same.

Your attitude will reflect what is truly going on in your heart. If you think yourself better than those around you, your attitude will reflect an arrogant, haughty, and pious mind-set. You can only hide your true attitude for so long. It is your front man that proclaims who you really are before you ever open your mouth. Your attitude is the agent of your reputation. No matter how successful, productive, intelligent, or capable you are or have been, your attitude will represent you in your current place.

Paul continually schools us in his writings concerning our attitude; he warns us not to think of ourselves more highly than we ought (Romans 12:3), and to treat everyone as better than yourself (Philippians 2:3). Paul employs us to stand firm, to serve Christ with the attitude of goodness, peace, and joy. To press on toward the Goal, and to have the attitude of Christ.

## 3 Components of Christ's Attitude

The standard or benchmark of our attitude is the attitude Christ had when He walked the earth. Jesus was fully God and fully man. In other words, He was tempted, suffered, felt pain, fought fatigue, struggled with fear, dealt with His emotions, experienced discouragement, loneliness, disappointment, and never once let any of the human experience conquer His attitude. We can align ourselves with Christ because He was fully man and did not consider His equality with God something to cling to.

Our attitude is so important to our daily lives. Attitude is what can make us or break us. Attitude is the difference between getting the job or not getting the job. I have said many times, I would rather work with someone who was a B or C student with a good attitude than one who got straight A's with a bad attitude. Remember, your appearance, personality, grades, or connections may get you into the room but your attitude is what is going to keep you in the room.

In Christ's attitude, we see three components we can implement in our lives:

**Servanthood**

What is the attitude of Christ? How do we know what that is? Paul writes further, "...He [Jesus] did not consider His equality with God something to be grasped but willingly emptied Himself." In other words, Jesus knows who He is but is not concerned with His position or title or authority. He steps aside from all that and becomes a man so that we might know God. Jesus is not concerned with His reputation or what others think about Him.

In a culture that is consumed with style and form, we can get caught up with who we are and making sure everyone knows it. We want titles, power, prestige, and image. Yet to have the attitude of Christ means to put all that aside and simply serve, simply obey, and simply love. Jesus understood who He was and where He came from and still washed the disciples' feet. In the book of John, chapter 13, we see the account of Jesus washing the feet of the disciples. In verse three, John writes that Jesus knew that His Father had put all authority under His feet. Jesus knew who and where He was, He knew where He was from, and that He would be going back to His Father. He knew where he was going. In other words, Jesus was a confident, powerful man who was self-assured. He had His marching orders. He was from good stock. He had an incredible inheritance, yet in light of who, what, and where He was, got up and washed His friends' feet. Now that's some attitude!

**Humility**

The foundation of a good attitude is humility. Remember, the standard of our attitude is Christ's attitude. He did not consider His equality with God something to be clung to. He was humble and not arrogant, confident and not conceited, full of spirit and not full of Himself.

The lesson learned in the upper room was Jesus's response to Peter when he refused to let Jesus wash his feet. Jesus looked at Peter very intently. I believe He paused, as if to say, *make sure you get this, understand what I am about to say,* and then stated, "Peter, if I don't wash your feet you have no part of Me." In other words, there is no claim to being a child of God without an attitude of humility and servanthood. There should never be a time where we reach a pentacle of position that we cannot, do not, or will not serve. Jesus set aside His position and served out of humility.

It may sound like Peter was being humble, yet in reality it was a false humility. If you have never been served before you may not understand this. One of the most humbling things in life is to be served. Jesus not only taught us to serve but also to be served. To be in a place of humility at all times no matter where you are in life. The child of God is a servant and at times served. Peter got the message. He said to Jesus to wash his head, hands and feet. In other words he wanted all of Jesus' attitude.

**Obedience**

Obedience is one of the hardest concepts to get into your spirit. We live in a culture of freedom and liberty, yet they have been defined as doing whatever you want, saying whatever you want, going wherever you want. The idea of obedience or submission is not in the vocabulary of the current culture.

Children, often times, are not made to obey for fear of damaging their psyche, or accusations of abuse. We have been told that our children can determine for themselves who they are, what they do, and who they will love. They can define for themselves their identity and their behavior.

The outcome of this "freedom" is a generation of adults who have no concept of obedience, delayed gratification, or submission. They have never had to perform or work for the reward because they were given participation trophies simply for showing up. Yet for the child of God, the foundational component of Christ's attitude is obedience.

Jesus is God, but He laid that down and submitted Himself to the will of His Father. Without a heart submitted to Christ, there can never be a Christlike attitude. This is true freedom and liberty because submission is a choice. No one is forcing you to obey. You have the freedom to obey. Every day when you proclaim, "...My attitude is like Christ's," you are saying, *I choose to obey. I choose to submit my life, my will, my thoughts to Christ.*

## 10 Attitude Habits

To have an attitude that is the same as Christ's, there are some habits to instill in your life. These ten habits, when implemented, will keep you focused on aligning your attitude with Him.

### 1. Be Grateful

Keep a gratitude journal or a gratitude section in your journal and every day write down what you are thankful for. Set a mental rule for your thinking that when you think, see, or meet with someone, you list the qualities, characteristics, or habits you are thankful for in them.

Write down the different experiences, relationships, and opportunities you are thankful for. List the blessings in your life and take a moment to simply give thanks. Start this way and continue throughout the day. Do not allow your mind to drift into entitlements, resentments, or a victim mentality. Keep focused on being grateful.

### 2. Define Your Mountains

There are no dead ends, only roadblocks, redirections, and detours. Remember, even the Apostle Paul was detoured by the enemy, but he still showed up. Do not fall into the attitude of cursing your purpose, vision, or dream due to the challenges in your life.

Define those challenges (mountains) for what they are. Every mountain you face will provide these three things:

- Training

You will get hands-on training for how to handle different situations.

- Preparing

You will be prepared for the coming adventure. You will receive new tools, equipment, and relationships in every mountain experience.

- Equipping

You will be equipped to use those tools. It is not effective to have all the tools in your belt if you do not know how to use them.

When you face mountains, pay attention to those around you or those who have faced similar ones. They are there to show you how to use the tools you are being given to face the mountain.

### 3. Accept Rejection

Understand that everyone faces rejection. Jesus was the chief of being rejected. He has even been called the chief cornerstone that the builders *rejected* (Psalm 118:22). Rejection is a part of life but does not have to be part of your attitude. Stop blaming your life on those who have rejected you, left you, or cursed you. Realize you are in very good company and move on.

Not everyone is going to like or believe in you, and that is OK. *It is OK!* For everyone who rejects you, there is One who will accept you. Just keep moving and do not quit. Remember, before you even start your day there is One who already accepts you and will never reject you. You are His Child!

**4. Describe your life with positive words**

How do you describe your life? Is it an adventure or a burden? Do you think life is happening to you or for you? Do you talk about how blessed you are, or how cursed you are? The words you use to describe yourself and your life are important. This is why you start each day with the Believer's Proclamation. Continually say, "I am a child of God. I am highly favored. Good things are coming my way. I will declare and proclaim, and never plead or beg."

God describes you as His child who He loves, cares for, and died for. Why would you ever describe yourself as anything less? Align your description of yourself and your life with God's description of yourself and your life. Watch how things begin to change in your life simply because you align with the Word of God.

When Jesus was facing the whip, hammer, and cross, He looked at Pilot and said, "My kingdom is not of this world..." He understood He was and is the King of kings. He understood who He was and why He was here. And you need to understand who you are, no matter what you are facing. You are a child of the Most High God.

**5. Change "*have* to" to "*get* to"**

This is a simple habit that has changed my life. I determined a long time ago that I don't *have* to do anything. I *get* to do everything. Every morning I wake up, I *get* to get out of bed. I *get* to go to the office. I *get* to go to church. I *get* to pay my bills. I *get* to mow the lawn or shovel the walks. I *get* to clean the house. I *get* to do this life. See how different this sounds: I *have* to get out of bed. I *have* to go to work. I *have* to pay the bills, and so on and so on. When you change your "*have* to" to "*get* to," there is a motivation that rises up in you. You will begin to face life with a much different passion.

### 6. Ban Complaining

One of the reasons the children of Israel spent forty years in the wilderness walking in circles is because of complaining. God told them that because of the attitude of complaining in their hearts, they would spend a generation in the wilderness before they were allowed to enter the promised land.

Is your complaining keeping you from the destiny God has for you? New adventures intended to take down giants, topple walls, and push back the forces of darkness in your family, friends, community, church, and yourself, can all be delayed because you have a complaining attitude.

If you continually complain, try this simple exercise:

- List all the things you complain about.
- Beside each complaint, write a "CN" beside the ones you cannot do anything about. Write a "C" beside the ones you can do something about.
- Determine to ban complaining from your mouth and mind for the next thirty days.

- Put your CNs on your prayer list for the next thirty days.
- Move your Cs to your task list for the next thirty days.

Remember, Jesus had every reason to complain, yet when He was going to the cross, He did not even open His mouth. He kept silent. He had already prayed about it. Sometimes your best attitude can be to stay silent.

### 7. Meditation (Breathe-Pause)

Do not kid yourself: there will be times when things seem to get out of control. Your finances, marriage, kids, or unforeseen illnesses consume every ounce of energy, focus, and time you have. When those times come and you feel negative emotions and a breakdown coming, pause and take a deep breath.

Learn to slow down and meditate. God instructed Joshua, in order to be courageous, he must meditate on His Word day and night. The word *meditate* here means to utter or muse. That means when it gets tough, take a breath, focus on the Word of God, and speak out the words God has given.

Some will avoid meditation because of the secular teachings of transcendental meditation. Don't forsake something simply because the world tries to take it and make it their own. They will teach you to empty your mind. That is not true meditation. True meditation is to focus, muse, ponder, and utter something.

Meditate on the fact that He will never leave you or forsake you. You are the head and not the tail, the top and not the bottom (Deuteronomy 28:13). Meditate on the fact that God has a plan to prosper you and to lift you up. Remember to focus on the reality that the enemy will come at you one way but will flee from you in seven different ways.

### 8. There is good in every tragedy

As I explained, our family went through a very tragic loss a few years ago. It was a traumatic time for all of us. It would have been easy to turn very dark and become discouraged. Yet we chose to see the good. The people in our lives came around us and loved us, cared for us, and stood in the gap when we couldn't stand at all.

Look past the tragedy to those who are doing good in the tragedy. The relief worker in the midst of the war-torn city. The one who gives food to the child starving in the shelter. There is righteousness in every tragedy. Focus on the righteous and allow God to use you as a beacon of light during dark times.

### 9. Be a problem solver. Not a notifier.

The other day, I saw a commercial on TV describing a monitoring service. The dentist looked into a man's mouth and said to the hygienist, "That is the worst cavity I have ever seen." He took off his gloves and headed out of the office. Confused, the man in the chair asked if the dentist was going to fill the decaying tooth. The dentist informed him that he was not a dentist, he was a *dental monitor*. He only notified when there was a problem; he didn't fix it.

Don't be someone who just points out the problem. Help figure out how to fix or solve it. Always looking for problems to identify and notify makes you a pessimist, and that's someone no one wants to be around. A child of God has the answer for the mountains, valleys, floods, and fires those in our lives go through.

It is not the attitude of Christ to point out the problem without offering a solution. It is, however, His attitude to come alongside and help solve the problem.

A problem solver is not looking at the problem; she is looking through the problem to find the solution. It's all about your focus. Being a problem solver does not mean you are not aware of the problems around you; you are just not fixated on it. Problem solvers look at problems as new challenges, experiences, and gateways to new opportunities, relationships, and successes.

**10. Go First and Eat Last**

Each morning, before you start your day, always determine to go first. Children of God always go first. The first to smile, the first to open the door, the first to say hi, and the first to give up your seat. Determine to serve first.

My son-in-law Jonathon was in the army. He told me that there would be times when he would not eat until very late at night or off schedule. When I asked him why, he said it was because he was the ranking officer. Officers in the military have a simple rule: they will never eat before their men eat, they will never sleep before their men sleep, they will never be served before their men are served. Jesus's attitude is that He came to serve and not be served. Think of that attitude. The King of kings—the let-there-be-light, water-walking, lion-silencing, bread-multiplying, resurrecting, grave-robbing, all-mighty-creative—says, *I will go first and eat last.*

Your attitude will determine what level you will rise to. Have the attitude of Christ and watch your life rise to levels you never thought possible. When you have the attitude of Christ, you will begin to hear what He is saying.

# Listen Up

## JESUS REPLIED, "BUT EVEN MORE BLESSED ARE ALL WHO HEAR THE WORD OF GOD AND PUT IT INTO PRACTICE." LUKE 11:28

"None so deaf as those that will not hear..." —Matthew Henry

### Hear the Word of God

What do you hear every day? What do you put into your mind through your eyes and ears? It is important to determine what you are going to hear every day. When you proclaim, "Today I will hear the word of God," you declare the filter by which you will hear everything else.

The amount of information we process in any given day is incredible. We no longer live in the industrial age. We have moved into the information age. In 2013, the average American household consumed 6.9 zettabytes of information. A zettabyte is beyond comprehension. It is basically one billion trillion bytes. To try to give some context to this, an exabyte is 1/1000 of a zettabyte or one billion gigabytes. One billion gigabytes is the equivalent of 5.1 million computer hard drives. To break it down even further, the average American consumed 34 gigabytes of information a day in 2008. Information consumption has increased by 6 percent each year from 1980 to 2008. That is an increase of 350 percent in 28 years. There is so much information we have to sift through to determine what is worthy of our attention. What is worthy of our observation.

With all that data, information, and opportunity streaming in every day, it can be increasingly difficult to determine what to listen to. The Bible tells us to be

> **Without a framework to filter everything we are bombarded with, we might go insane.**

very careful who we listen to (Colossians 2:8). The philosophies and human reasoning of today can and does cloud our mind. As a child of God, you must be careful to establish filters and frameworks to weed out what is human reasoning that will lead to death and what is divine direction that leads to life. The importance of a framework or filter has never been more real than it is today. You have to choose not to read, listen, or watch most of what comes through each channel in your life.

## Hear it

There is incredible privilege that comes to those who choose to hear the Word of God. Jesus was talking to a group of people and a woman came to Him and said, "Your mother is so blessed to have had you as a son." Jesus basically said thank you for the compliment, but actually those who hear the Word of God are blessed. He wanted to make sure that the favor of God was not simply bestowed on a few chosen who were given a designation like Mary, but *anyone* who chooses to hear His Word.

Today, as you hear the Word of God for your life, you are highly blessed. It is a true blessing to hear the Word of God. Don't take that for granted. There are entire groups of people who have never heard the Word of God. The wonderful message that the Creator of the universe loves you so much has never been heard by some living on this planet. Could you imagine, not knowing, hearing, or learning about the incredible Word of God?

## Live it

We are so blessed to hear the Word of God. But the true favor and blessing from God comes when we **live** the Word of God. Jesus was very clear that we are blessed to hear the Word of God. Jesus also made it clear that just hearing it will not bring the favor and blessings that the Word of God points to without behavior, action, and submission to what it teaches (Luke 11:28).

Every child learns the lesson of hearing and obeying, usually the hard way. We cannot simply hear God's words and not let them influence our lives. We have to apply what we hear every day. Application is the secret to any successful mission. If we don't apply these words to our life, what use is the Word of God? Jesus said you are blessed if you hear the Word of God *and* observe it. It is observing that we lose sight of so many times.

Observing means to pay attention, focus on, and to guard. The Word of God will keep you safe if you apply its principles and teachings to your life. The Apostle James commented on how deceptive it is to only be a hearer of the Word and not one who acts on it (James 1:22) It is like looking into a mirror and seeing yourself, only to walk away and not remember what you look like. A child of God knows what they look like, act like, and talk like. Observing the Word of God is to apply it, not violate it. When we apply the Word to our lives, it is a guard to keep us safe. The Word guides us to say the right things, do the right things, and go to the right places, all at the right time.

Your ways become pure and your direction is no longer in confusing darkness. You suddenly have a perspective that is accurate and affective. There is a sense within that you understand the workings of this world and can make decisions that lead to success. When you begin to hear and observe the Word of God, you have an innate ability to make decisions that seem right, even when on the surface don't look right.

## Captivate thoughts

We are to take every thought captive. (2 Corinthians 10:5) That means every bad *and* good thought. Not just the bad thoughts. Many times, I have heard this passage of scripture used to warn the hearer to take the bad thoughts captive, but Paul is telling us to take *every* thought captive.

Hearing creates thoughts, thoughts lead to mind-sets, and mind-sets lead to behavior. Whatever you are hearing in a day has the potential to determine how you will behave over a lifetime. Over time, hearing the same things again and again will imprint on your mind, and you will begin to think the same thing. As I stated earlier, Paul said to take every thought captive. Not just the bad thoughts, not just the thoughts that are dark, condemning, and full of doubt, but every thought. In other words, we are always to be focused on what we are hearing every day. Don't just mindlessly sit in your car, recliner, or at work and listen to whatever is coming through your channels. Focus on it and ask yourself, is this something I want to use to influence my thought life?

Just because something you are hearing is good or neutral doesn't mean you should be filling your mind with it. Is what you are hearing going to inspire the most productivity in your life? Can you use what you are hearing to build up those around you? Do not sacrifice the best simply because you are capturing the good.

**Frame**

Each morning you wake up, you have a new day and new opportunities before you. How is this day going to be framed? All the data that comes into your world has to be funneled into a mainframe. Just like data into a computer, there are hard parameters that will determine how the data is to be handled. You are the mainframe. You are the hard drive. What can you handle and what is too much? Just as you know how much memory, storage, and software your computer has on its mainframe, you have the responsibility to know what you can handle, how much storage and memory you have. Trying to pack so much information and data into your life can be the same as trying to put too much in a computer hard drive. The systems start to fail. The basic operations no longer work.

My wife was having problems opening her email on her phone. Every time she tapped on the mail icon to open the app, it closed down. A notice popped up: "*Your storage is full.*" There was too much data in the phone's hard drive. The basic systems of the phone, like checking emails, making calls, texting, communicating with her leadership team, family, and friends couldn't happen because there was too much data on the mainframe.

The same thing happens to us when we do not understand how our mainframe works. When we neglect to determine what our body, mind, and spirit can handle, our basic systems break down. Do not neglect what your mind, body, and spirit can handle.

**Focus**

The amount of information streaming into your life each day is mind-boggling. The key to disseminating all this information is to focus. It is the same practice you use to eat right and to be disciplined with your finances. You have to pay attention, take every thought captive. The tendency is to let each day go by without being aware of what is being delivered into your life. The billboard you drive by each day, the radio station that is always on in your vehicle, the media you watch, or the newspaper that is delivered either to your front door or your newsfeed all provide a message.

Be proactive in your hearing. Start each day hearing the Word of God. Listen to sermons that will reinforce the Word of God in your life. Subscribe to podcasts, read books, listen to music that uplifts and explains the Word of God. Get a Bible app for your phone that will speak the Word of God to you. Set a goal to read the Bible through every year. Change it up by reading the Bible in a different translation each year. Pick a different Bible reading plan. One year, read the Bible in ninety days, then read it in chronological order. You get the point; you have to focus and create a plan to hear the Word of God every day.

Be balanced in what you are hearing each day. Do not just read or listen to the Bible. You also have to know what is going on in the world. Believers are Issachar people (1 Chronicles 12:32). Issachar was one of Jacob's twelve sons. As his family grew, it was noted of the sons of Issachar that they understood the times and knew what Israel should do. Believers understand the times and know what the church is supposed to do.

You need to be relevant and current in your understanding of what is going on around you. Listen to the news, be connected to the community, read and know the popular culture. It is important for believers to be balanced in what they hear. Too much of one thing will cause you to be out of balance.

**Filter**

Our mind, body, and spirit is the mainframe. The software, or operating system we put in the mainframe, to run the system, is the filter. What is your operating system? For the believer, the operating system for our lives is the Word of God. We focused on the Word of God being the foundation earlier, so I will not go into much depth here, other than to say, the Word of God is the filter through which to screen everything.

**Action**

Hearing is an action. Hearing literally means to consider what is being heard. So many times, we let things go in one ear and out the other without considering what is being said. The pious, prideful religious leaders of his day did not consider what Jesus was saying because it was so contrary to their profitable way of living. It seemed He was speaking a different language they could not understand. Many times, when the believer hears the Word of God, there is a moment in which he or she has the choice whether to consider or ignore it.

The temptation to ignore what you are hearing comes when you are either being confronted concerning your behavior or confused and don't understand. Many times, the Word of God is very confrontational concerning behavior. Jesus was usually confrontational with those religious leaders who knew better but refused to change. The other temptation is to disregard what we hear because we don't understand. Entire churches, denominations, and groups have formed because there are sections of the Word of God they do not regard at all. It seems that if a portion of scripture doesn't fit in their interpretation, understanding, or explanation, it is ignored. If the Word of God creates more work or makes things messy, that portion is deemed irrelevant.

Many years ago, I was pastoring and realized we were not leading the church according to the way the Word of God prescribed us to. I began to do an in-depth study, as I considered what I was hearing in the Word of God, I made some changes. This brought about actions from some leaders that were not at all positive. There was one day when I was asked to come to a leader's home to discuss the matter. I brought my study and the Bible with me, which I thought was a good idea. As the conversation escalated into a discussion and then a disagreement, I pointed to the Word of God and said, "It is all in here. I'm not suggesting anything that this book doesn't prescribe." One of the leaders looked at the Bible, slid it off the table, and said, "I don't care what that says; this is not the way we do it." I learned something that day. If you are going to hear only a portion of the Word of God, at one point you will have to disregard the whole Word of God.

It is called the Word of God, not the *words* of God. It is complete and cannot be divided up and parceled out to make it palatable and conforming to our behavior and understanding. Believers are transformed by the Word of God, and even if you do not understand every part, you can still conform and let the Holy Spirit reveal through your faith.

# Just Do It!

## "TRY TO PLEASE THEM ALL THE TIME, NOT JUST WHEN THEY ARE WATCHING YOU. AS SLAVES OF CHRIST, DO THE WILL OF GOD WITH ALL YOUR HEART." EPHESIANS 6:6

> "Start by doing what's necessary; then do what's possible; and suddenly you are doing the impossible."—Francis of Assisi

### Do the Will of God

I determined a long time ago not to be just a hearer of the Word of God but also a doer. Doing is the sign of your belief. What you do comes from what you believe. As a child of God, your faith is the springboard for your action. Do not fall into the trap of action-based Christianity. Your actions are not the foundation of your salvation. That is not possible. Your faith is the foundation of your actions.

I have heard people say if they just prayed longer, fed the hungry more, memorized more scripture, served more in church, or told more people about Jesus, maybe God would love them more. All those things are good, and every child of God should be doing each of those actions with passion. But a works-based mentality will only lead to frustration and failure. God is not going to love you any more or any less due to your actions. He is your Father, He simply loves you. There is no loving more or less with God. His love does not go up and down according to your attitude, level of service, or amount of giving. The same as with your own children. You do not love them less because they are not obeying you or love them more because their attitude is right. You simply love them.

If your faith is based on your actions, you will expect people to notice what you are doing. You will need attention, credit, and thank-you's. Notice what Paul says: "work hard, but not just to please the masters when they are looking..." The kind of living Paul is speaking of here is not gratification or attention-based. We should not be doing these things because someone is watching or rewarding us.

Faith-based action comes from your passionate love for your Father and the things He loves. You could not stop *doing* if you tried. Your actions quite literally come from your heart, your very passion. No one has to keep reminding you to get up and do the will of God. You act according to the Spirit that is in you.

When you apply the Will and Word of God to your life, you begin to live a life of excellence. Because God's will for you is excellence.

## Spirit of Excellence (whole heart)

"Whatever your hand finds to do, do it with excellence and all your heart" (Ecclesiastes 9:10). This is complete passion. There is nothing I love more than to listen to someone talk about something they are passionate about. Several years ago, I experienced passion while getting my car's oil changed. I frequented this place every few months to make sure I would have a certain mechanic service my car because he was so passionate about cars, engines, and taking care of them. He would show me the new filters that came in. The entire time, he would talk about how a well-running engine is the prettiest sound ever. I could listen to him and watch him do his job for hours. Why? Not because I'm in to engines and cars, I'm in to passion. I wasn't listening to his subject as much as I was captivated by his passion.

This kind of excellence is sourced by the very breath you breathe. The word for *heart* in Ecclesiastes 9:10 means *life breath* or *life source*. It is the very place where God breathed in you and you became a living being. As a child of God, you bring your very life force to doing His will. He breathed life into you, and now you use that life to do the will of He who gave you that breath.

This is no haphazard way of living; no, you put your all into doing! Everything you do flows from a place of passion and excellence.

**This child-of-God life is all-consuming and all-encompassing.**

Many times, I have seen people allow the desire for excellence to stop them from doing something. They will say they can't do it with excellence, so they won't even try. This is the wrong understanding of excellence. It is not an outward standard. If that were the case, there would always be an excuse not to try.

Excellence is an inward standard. Notice the standard of excellence Jesus applied in the story of the talents (Matthew

25:14-28). The master was leaving for a time and gave some money to each of His servants: five thousand to one, two thousand to another, and one thousand to the last. The first two servants invested and doubled their money. The last servant was fearful of losing the money, so he buried his portion. When the Master came back, he received the report of their work. If excellence is outward, each would have been judged by the Master's standard and rewarded accordingly. However, the first two did the best with what they had and were rewarded the same, partners in the kingdom. The third, however, did not even do the least of what he was capable. He was judged by what he had *and* what he could have done, not by what he did not have.

Excellence is determined by your level of effort, understanding, and passion. Do the best you can, with all your understanding, resources, knowledge, and skill. Then you will hear the Master say, "Well Done!"

## Spirit of Generosity

Feeding the poor, clothing the naked, housing the homeless, healing the sick, speaking life into the lifeless, and hope into the hopeless: these are the signs and actions of those who do the will of God. When we do the will of God, it begins to transform our families, communities, schools, and churches.

> **Can you imagine the power of an entire group of people determining to do the will of the all-powerful, all-knowing, everywhere God?**

Everything you do should flow from the will of God. Therefore, His will is the foundation of your action, passion, and purpose.

Once you better understand the priority of generosity in the will of the Father, you will focus on being generous through action.

One of the questions I am most often asked is how do I know what the will of God is for my life? Finding the will of God seems to lead to much confusion and conflict in the life of the believer. Who to marry? Where to go to school? What career to choose? All of these questions seem to consume us. But the scripture is very clear on what the true will of God is in our lives. The will of God is to care for the orphan and widow, love others as our self, walk humbly, love mercy, act justly. These are the basics, and once you have mastered the spirit of generosity in your life, God will begin to open the doors and windows of opportunity and blessings will flow. Realize that God has already prescribed what His will is. Once you do His will, He will add the rest.

**Spirit of Action**

Believers are not only hearers but also doers. Believers are people of action. A child of God gets up every day and takes on the day. The phrase Carpe diem, seize the day, used by Horace, the Roman poet, is to convey the idea we should act now, make the most of now. Do not wait or put effort into tomorrow. When you connect your listening with doing, the Gospel takes on an entirely new effectiveness. Whole neighborhoods, cities, states, nations, economies, groups, and governments could be affected. As a child of God, you are to be a person of action. Don't be someone who has the reputation of all words and no action. The Church is full of people who just talk or sit and listen but do not stand up and act.

I love how Eugene Peterson interprets Colossians 3:1, 2 (MSG):

"So if you're serious about living this new resurrection

life with Christ, act like it. Pursue the things over which Christ presides. Don't shuffle along, eyes to the ground, absorbed with the things right in front of you. Look up, and be alert to what is going on around Christ—that's where the action is. See things from H*is* perspective."

As a child of God, you proclaim not only the title of being a child of God but also the lifestyle of a child of God.

## Spirit of Application

Proverbs 23:12 says, "Apply your heart..." The word *apply* in this scripture means to attack. The destiny and discipline God has placed in you as His child needs to be attacked and brought to reality. Attack with passion, power, and purpose. Whenever an army attacks, they do so with a plan. It's easy to say words, but living those words is much more difficult. Application is the key to any successful mission, vision, or plan.

**God has placed in you an incredible destiny, an amazing mission, and a victorious vision. All you have to do is apply what He has placed in you to your daily life.**

**Without application, the greatest missions become the poorest wishes, the saddest would haves, and the sorriest could haves, instead of the greatest triumphs.**

A child of God does not take the words and Will of God as theory but literally applies them to his or her heart. As you continue to walk as a child of God, you will become a person of application. Application is the key to success as a child of God. The believer shows they truly believe according to how they apply the words. You cannot say you are a believer or a child of God and not apply Christ's teaching to your life. It is impossible.

# Convicted Lifestyle

> "AND HE, WHEN HE COMES, WILL CONVICT THE WORLD CONCERNING SIN AND RIGHTEOUSNESS AND JUDGMENT..." (NASB)
> JOHN 16:8

"Let us go forward in this battle fortified by conviction that those who labour in the service of a great and good cause will never fail." —Owen Arthur

"There can be no great courage where there is no confidence or assurance, and half the battle is in the conviction that we can do what we undertake." —Orison Swett Marden

## Today I will be convicted

That is a difficult proclamation. It literally means to be corrected, exposed, admonished, reproved, or punished. In a day when it seems that we want to be encouraged and spurred on with uplifting words, don't lose sight of the fact that you may need to be corrected. There is a temptation to let pride filter and be convinced there is no need for you to be convicted. God is a good Father and wants the best for you. Part of that best for you is discipline. Remember, the best fathers also are the best disciplinarians.

No one wants to be around an undisciplined child. They are demanding, disrespectful, and arrogant. Many years ago, I scheduled a meeting and ordered refreshments for the gathering. I walked into the kitchen, and there stood my boss's son with his mouth full of doughnuts from the tray. When I asked him what he was doing, he said, "My dad's the boss. I can do whatever I want."

Many times, I see those who claim to be a child of God and have no discipline in their lives. They may not say it, but they act like they're the boss's kid and can do whatever they want. In the book of Hebrews, it is stated that if you don't accept the discipline, correction, or conviction of God, you really are not His child; you are illegitimate. God wants the best for you, which is why He disciplines you. Take this seriously, and don't give up when you feel the correction of your Heavenly Father. If He does not correct you, that means He does not love you, and that is impossible. He loves you so much!

Proclaiming you will be convicted today is a sign of maturity. Those who accept the discipline of the Father and correct their ways grow up. There is a difference in growing up or growing old in the kingdom of God. I have seen many who have been in the kingdom of God for many years, if not decades, and yet their actions, tantrums, and immaturity seem to indicate they have only been a child of God a few short months. On the other hand, I have witnessed those who are new to being a child of God who have yielded to His discipline. Their maturity and level of living is head and shoulders above those who refuse to yield to the conviction of the Holy Spirit.

## Process of Conviction

Conviction is a process. It is not something that happens instantly and the change is immediate. This is why it can seem like being a child of God is difficult. The process can be long and hard. At times it can feel like there is no progress at all. Let the work of the Holy Spirit continue in your life and do not fall into the world of condemnation.

### Private to Public

God's discipline comes in different forms. His conviction always follows a process of private to public. God will convict you privately of attitudes, actions, habits, or relationships that are contrary to His ways. During those times, He expects you to correct those ways and continue walking your path to full maturity in Him. If you yield to His correction, you will experience freedom and deliverance. If you do not yield and continue walking the same path, He will continue to bring correction. Each time you refuse, the correction will be more public, until the time in which your fall will be very public and all will see.

## Word of God

The Father will bring correction to us through His Word. We have already focused on our foundation being the Word of God, so I will not spend too much time on that here. Just know there will be times when you are unaware that what you are saying, doing, or connecting with is contrary to the ways of the Father. He will reveal those to you through His Word. Remember, the Bible states that people die for the lack of knowledge (Hosea 4:6).

The word *die* in Hosea 4:6 means destroyed. It means to be cut off, undone, or to cease. In other words, if you do not yield to the Word of God, you will be cut off from His blessing, protection, and provision. This is not simply a level of ignorance but a rejection of the knowledge. It seems the trend of today is to accept only certain portions of scripture. Usually, what is accepted is the blessing, provision, vision, and grace portions, and those are certainly promised. As a child of God, you are required to accept the whole teaching, truth, and Word of God. Realize there is the expectation of the Father that you know His Word and accept all of it without rejecting any of it. Jesus came to earth full of grace (blessing) and truth (standard). You cannot have one without the other. You cannot have prosperity without problems or blessing without burden.

## Fathers and Brothers—Mothers and Sisters

God will also bring correction to you as His child from fathers and brothers and mothers and sisters in your life. It never ceases to amaze me how God will bring people into my life to sharpen, mentor, and mold me. I am honored to have traveled through many years with friends and fathers who guide me and continue to hold me accountable in my attitudes, actions, and behaviors.

> **Part of living a convicted life is to put people in your life who know you, love you, and are willing to tell you when you are on track and when you start to veer off.**

Determine today to have a group of mentors whom you have given permission to ask you the tough questions. These can be the board of directors for your life. These can be men or women who are at different stages in life.

## Humility

Being under conviction requires you to walk in humility. You are never beyond correction. This is why the Bible warns us that pride goes before a fall. The pride is the refusal to submit to His loving discipline. A fall happens when we ignore the discipline, correction, and conviction. God wants to deal with you in the privacy of your heart. But if your heart is filled with pride and arrogance and you do not deal with it, He will deal with you in the public arena.

## Standard

Have convictions in life. I have many opinions but few convictions. Opinions change but convictions do not. Opinions are subject to circumstances and seasons. I will die for my convictions.

When you proclaim you are a child of God and will be convicted, you are proclaiming you will live within the boundaries of His house. Entering into the kingdom of God assumes you will live according to the convictions of the Holy Spirit. When you sense the leading of the spirit, you will listen. When you feel the prodding, that something is not the way it should be, you correct your course.

The life of conviction is a life ruled by Holy Spirit discernment. Conviction is to know the difference between sin and righteousness. This is what the Holy Spirit does in our life. He comes to convict the world in matters of sin and righteousness.

Understanding that there is a day of judgment and you will be judged according to the convictions of the Holy Spirit is what leads us to being challenged.

# Face the Challenge

> "ANYONE WHO MEETS A TESTING CHALLENGE HEAD-ON AND MANAGES TO STICK IT OUT IS MIGHTY FORTUNATE. FOR SUCH PERSONS LOYALLY IN LOVE WITH GOD, THE REWARD IS LIFE AND MORE LIFE." JAMES 1:12 (MSG)

"The ultimate measure of a man is not where he stands in moments of comfort and convenience, but where he stands at times of challenge and controversy." —Martin Luther King Jr.

## Today I will be Challenged

Life is full of challenges, and the life of the believer is made stronger when we face the challenges and prevail. Sometimes the challenge we face is God's way of testing to see if we are ready for the next phase of walking with Him. God has such an incredible life in store for you, filled with blessings, influences, and prosperity. If you are not tested in the fire, you will not be ready for the responsibility and pressure of the new level of blessing. Many times, I see people promoted in their careers before they are ready. It is difficult to watch as those who have not stood the test, fail. The Word of God is very clear that we should be careful when we seek positions of influence, leadership, or prosperity because once the promotion happens, the pressure and stress not only increase, they multiply.

Don't be fooled by the thought that once you have become a child of God you will never face any challenges or have any troubles. This life is always going to be challenging. We will face challenges that have the potential of taking us out of the game or propel us further on into a greater level of it.

A challenge is something or someone calling you out to test your position, hear your side of the story, or to defend your place. Many years ago, it was common to challenge someone to a duel. One of the Founding Fathers of the United States, Alexander Hamilton, was killed in a duel. Being challenged for something you say or do is what forces the child of God to become the man or woman God has called them to be.

To be ready for the challenges of the day, you have to be very clear on who you are and what you are capable of. You are a child of God. When you are convicted and confident in who you are and what you can handle, you can face any challenge.

There are two different kinds of challenges you will face: giant challenges and God challenges. Each come from a completely different direction. Both have completely different outcomes. You need to learn how to discern the difference, because both feel like they are from the same place and have the same end in mind. Let's learn how to tell the difference.

## The Giant Challenge

The Israelites had to face bigger giants, heavier fortified cities, and greater threats in the promised land than they did in the wilderness. I have seen many people stumble and fail because they were sure that once they crossed into their promised land—that promotion, marriage, kids, financial security, committing their life to Christ would be the answer for a stress- and trouble-free life. But that is not the case. Jesus was very clear about this in the book of John: "But, take heart, in this world you will have trouble, but I have overcome the world"—Jesus.

Sometimes it feels like becoming a child of God is just the beginning of the challenges and troubles. There are times in everyone's life when they will face challenges. These challenges come in many different forms. Believers face challenges every day. When you proclaim that "today...I will be challenged," you are accepting the reality of life. You are acknowledging the fact that today, you will have the opportunity to stand up and be firm in who you are and what you can do.

Every day, I see people who proclaim the incredible truth and privilege of being challenged. They are regular moms and dads, students and teachers, bank presidents and janitors, police officers and firemen. People just like you, slaying the giants in their lives.

**Just like the Israelites, you will defeat the giants, lay waste to the walls around your provision, and scatter the threats of the enemy.**

There was a young man who visited the battlefield of the Israelite army. Israel and the Philistines were in a standoff. The young man's name was David. Little did he know that when his father asked him to take some food and supplies to his brothers on the front line, he was going to face a challenge that would be a defining moment in his life. Remember, each challenge you face could be the defining moment that catapults you into your destiny. This was David's defining moment. He had the opportunity to run, hide, or simply go back to his comfort zone. That was not David's style or character. He knew he had to face his giant. It was by no coincidence he was in this predicament.

You may start your day the way you have always started it. The routine is set, the schedule is planned, and you are on your way. Then something happens, and you are faced with a giant standing in front of you. What are you going to do? What is your next step? Be a David, face the giant, slay it, and step into your destiny. Don't curse the giant or complain about it. The giant may very well be positioned by God to catapult you into your destiny.

Realize that no matter how right you live and how simply you walk, you will face trouble; you will face giants. Jesus was very clear in that. He tells us, "Don't be dismayed, in this world you will face troubles, but do not fear, I have overcome the world" (the source and environment of the challenges and troubles). (John 16:33).

When you face times of trouble you are challenged to stay strong and diligent. The word *trouble* means to be pressed, in dire straits, under undue pressure or stress. This world can offer all kinds of stress and pressure. Financial, career, relationships, success and failure, reputation are just some of what can be challenging in your life. Remember, when David defeated Goliath, the rest of the army ran. All the giants in that army ran. When one giant is slayed in your life, the rest tend to fall as well.

You might be facing a giant called disease, poverty, lack, fear, discouragement, death, depression. Or your giant might be intimidation, generational curses, addiction, or shame. That giant is taunting you and reminding you of your past. He is trying to convince you that his weapons and insults are real and can destroy you. But they cannot.

Remember what David said when he faced his giant, "You come at me with insults and human weapons, but I come in the name of the Lord God of Israel." David was saying, *You might be big and bad, but not bigger and badder than my Dad. He is the Lord of all. He will deliver you into my hands.* That day, the giant fell and David prevailed.

**This day, proclaim you are a child of God and your giant will fall and you will be victorious.**

## The God Challenge

Jesus challenged the level of commitment of an influential young man who wanted to know how to follow Him, how to be a child of God. Jesus laid down the challenge. He called him out. We cannot make the mistake of thinking that once we have become a child of God, we no longer face a God who leaves us alone. Christ wants the best for you. He wants you to continue to develop into an incredible giant killer. So He challenges us every day. You may feel you are being challenged by the giant, but in reality, God is challenging you to lay down something or take on something that is going to open doors and move you to the next level in the Kingdom. We are constantly moving from Glory to Glory (2 Corinthians 3:18). The God challenges are the *to* between the glories. Those are difficult times that feel like they are Giant challenges rather than God challenges.

God challenges are designed to show you and God if you are ready for the next level. Abraham faced an incredible challenge that he passed and was able to raise up

> **Giant challenges are designed to destroy you and God challenges are designed to develop you.**

the next generation. God told Abraham to take his son to be sacrificed. Isaac was the son God had given to Abraham and Sarah in their old age. The vision, dream, future, and reason for their being. Abraham did exactly what God told him to do, and at the very last minute. God stopped Abraham from sacrificing his son. The words of the Lord of Hosts were very telling: "...Now I know you fear God..." (Genesis 22:11). God allowed Abraham to go to the brink of sacrificing Isaac to see if he could be trusted. Sometimes, the conflict you are going through is to allow God to see if you can be trusted with what He has given you.

Approximately 450 years later, Moses is given a challenge to speak to a rock in order to produce sweet water. Moses struck the rock instead. His anger, impatience, and pride got the best of him. The result: Moses was not allowed to enter into the promised land. He was commanded by God to appoint Joshua as the one to lead them in. What is interesting about this account is, just months before, God had instructed Moses to strike the rock with his staff and sweet water would flow.

Each one of these accounts of God challenges reveal the importance of being challenged. You never know what challenge God is using to propel you to the next level. That is why you have faith to move mountains and you trust God as your Father and you as His child.

Be willing to lay down the vision, dream, expectation, reputation, or relationship on the altar of sacrifice. When God calls you to speak instead of act, don't let your frustration get the best of you. Your words and actions today could be the very thing that release blessings on the next generation, or keep you out of the promised land altogether.

It is in the *to* times when we cannot give up. God is doing His work. It is during this time that we are face-to-face with Him, as if looking in a mirror, becoming more and more like Him. He is very present at this time. The old ways of doing things become obsolete. We become more and more filled with His Spirit. We are created in His image. Now we begin to take on His likeness. Your actions, reactions, and responses are more and more like His. Your life becomes brighter and brighter as His Spirit takes over more and more of your life.

# Changed for a Purpose

"DON'T BECOME SO WELL-ADJUSTED TO YOUR CULTURE THAT YOU FIT INTO IT WITHOUT EVEN THINKING. INSTEAD, FIX YOUR ATTENTION ON GOD. YOU'LL BE CHANGED FROM THE INSIDE OUT. ROMANS 12:2 (MSG)

"To improve is to change; to be perfect is to change often." —Winston Churchill

### Today I will be Changed

Every day you proclaim to be changed, you are declaring that you will not be pressured into the ways of the world. You are changed from what you used to be into what God has called you to be. The believer's life is not one where God fits into your way of living. As we discussed in earlier chapters, we are to align ourselves with the ways God intends for us to live. We do not try to fit Christianity into the culture of the world. This is not just a proclamation of words but also change. God doesn't want to simply fit into the way you live life. He wants to come in and radically change your life. To bring out the best in you, to develop you into an incredibly mature individual who will make a difference.

Many times, I see people make a declaration for Jesus Christ, but there is no change in their life. They still have the same thoughts, same actions, same relationships, same habits, same routines. No change at all. The life of the believer is such a radical shift from what the world views as an acceptable lifestyle, there must be change.

The focus of the change is you. You are the focus of the change you proclaim, not anyone else. Many times, we go through life thinking, *if my boss, spouse, kids, mom, or dad, would change, everything would be better.* Our prayers center around everyone in our lives who we deem need to change. We pray, *Lord, change my wife/husband; then I would be able to serve you better.*

Many years ago, a family went through a very devastating failure. From everyone's perspective, it seemed the son had made many unwise choices. The father was very upset and didn't know what to do. As a true man of God, the dad would always pray about every situation that needed divine guidance. I remember him telling me how he would pray, *God change my son.* It seemed like a good prayer. The son was really struggling and needed God to guide him onto a different path. In the middle of the prayer, the Lord stopped him and said, *If you really want your son to change you need to first change yourself.*

We can get into such a rut of thinking everything and everyone else needs to change, never realizing we need to change. We can actually be the change the world needs. Every day, you proclaim, *Today, I am changed,* you are reminded to focus on the change that needs to come into your life and let God deal with the changes that need to come in the lives of those around you. You may even find out that once the change God wants in your life is accomplished, those around you really don't need to change all that much.

There is no point to Christianity if it doesn't make a change in your life. There is no such thing as a Christian in name only, or one who creates their own belief system and calls it Christianity. The Bible talks about a day when people will have a form of godliness but will deny the power (2 Timothy 3:5). In other words, they will claim to be Christians, and even go through the motions, but never change. That is unacceptable for a child of God. Each day you proclaim you will be changed, you are giving God authority to change you. You are saying, *I will submit to being changed, to live as a child of God.*

Change is difficult to accomplish, but you can do it. Sometimes the change might be in a relationship, a career, a thought process, a habit, or a language. We get into a rut in how we live and it is difficult to get out. In the wilderness of Alaska, the roads are quite primitive, and in the summer, the roads thaw and become pliable. As vehicles go down the same path day after day, ruts begin to form. Once winter comes, the roads freeze and the ruts become solid and hard as concrete. A sign at the beginning of the road states, "'Choose your rut carefully; you will be in it for the next fifty miles." Life is the same way; the ruts we choose are very difficult to get out of.

The change may not be changing something that is dark or wrong in your life. It may be something that is no longer effective. There are times in life that we have been on a road that God no longer wants us on and we need to make a change. What was good for you a decade ago may no longer be effective. The life of the believer needs to be flexible, ready for anything that comes and willing to change. I remember when my children were getting older and I had to change the way I disciplined them. The way you correct a two-year-old is much different from the way you correct a seven-, ten-, or sixteen-year-old. Yet often we do not change our way of doing things.

> **Once you start proclaiming every day that you are changed, you are declaring that you will not stay in the rut that is leading to death, destruction, or despair.**

To stay changed and not slip back into our old ways, we must continually think about our culture and lifestyle. The culture of this world wants to put a lid on you. It wants to keep you confined and constantly tell you what you cannot do. The word *conform* in Romans 12:2 means to be pressed or squeezed into a mold. This is pressure from the outside. The word *transform* in Romans 12:2 means to be changed from the inside. When you proclaim you are changed, you are declaring God has the power to transform you from the inside out. You are full of His Spirit. When you are pressed and squeezed by the outside forces of this world, the force in you is greater, and you will not conform.

PART III

# Practice of Proclamation

*Live the Believer's Proclamation*

# Name of Jesus

"THEREFORE GOD EXALTED HIM TO THE HIGHEST PLACE AND GAVE HIM THE NAME THAT IS ABOVE EVERY NAME, THAT AT THE NAME OF JESUS EVERY KNEE SHOULD BOW, IN HEAVEN AND ON EARTH AND UNDER THE EARTH." PHILIPPIANS 2:9,10

> "To holy people the very Name of Jesus is a Name to feed upon, a Name to transport. His Name can raise the dead and transfigure and beautify the living." —John Henry Newman

## In Jesus' Name

2 Corinthians 1:20 says that every promise made by God is a yes in Christ. In other words, when we end the proclamation with, "In Jesus' Name…" we are saying that the promises we have declared here today are yeses *because* of Jesus Christ. There is not one

promise you proclaim in the Word of God that is a no for you. They are all yes, no matter how many you need to proclaim. Today, as you declare, "in the Name of Jesus," healing, restoration, freedom, reconciliation, financial blessing, salvation, deliverance, victory, clarity, promotion, purpose, conviction, encouragement, knowledge, resources, empowerment will come into your life!

When you say, "in the Name of Jesus," you are calling on the author of the promise. The authority of the One who made the promise. These are not simply your proclamations of what you hope to be or would like. No, the Creator of all has made these promises to you, and you say, "in the Name of Jesus."

When my twin granddaughters, MiCali and MiKayla, were two years old, they learned to pray. At the dinner table, we would say, *let's pray*, and they would bow their heads and fold their hands and say, "in Jesus' Name, Amen." That was it. My son, Nathan, had some health issues for about four months at that time. Each night, Victoria would say to the girls, *Let's pray for Uncle Nate*. They would each bow their head in their crib and say *In the Name of Jesus, amen!* Those two little ones, in their simple faith, understood a principle that we many times miss. All you need is, *In the Name of Jesus!*

Peter and John were two of the twelve disciples of Jesus who followed and learned directly from Him for over three years. Once Jesus was crucified, buried, raised from the dead, and went back to heaven, Peter and John continued the work Jesus started. They were going to church (synagogue) one day, and a paralyzed man called out to them,

**You do not need money, education, fame, or a big following. All you need is the authority of Jesus.**

asking if they could spare some money. This beggar could not work and therefore was hungry and needed money to buy food. Peter and John stopped. Peter told the man to look at them, and then he said, "Silver and Gold I do not have, but what I do have I will give you." At that moment, he got up and started dancing and praising God. The man didn't need monetary assistance. He needed a miracle.

Too many times, we do not stop to take care of the need right in front of us because we do not look past what the request is. This man was asking for money, but what he needed was healing. Other needs we ask for include education, power, security, safety, food, clothing, and the list can go on and on. We cannot always fill those requests; we may not have the education, the resources, or the ability. Yet as a child of God, do not simply look at the request; look past it to what is truly needed and give what you have. You have the ultimate authority in the world, In the Name of Jesus....

There is no other Name or author who has more power or authority in heaven or on earth. The Bible says that every knee will bow and every tongue confess that Jesus is Lord (Philippians 2:10). He is the power and authority over all and therefore can back up this proclamation.

> **The Name of Jesus is higher than any other name. At the Name of Jesus, the enemy has to run from you.**

There is a story in the Bible of a man confronting Jesus. This man was full of over a thousand demons, was tormented, and terrorized the local villages. He lived in a graveyard, and as Jesus approached the area, this tormented man ran up and begged Jesus not to cast him into hell. This was not the man talking but the demons. They were afraid of Jesus. They knew that Jesus, at His command, could relegate them back to the deepest, darkest hole in hell. They pleaded, begged, and bartered with Jesus.

You have the authority and power to cast out demons, heal the sick, raise the dead, bring light to the darkness, release to the captive, hope to the hopeless, and freedom to the prisoner. When you bow your knee and confess that Jesus is Lord, the inheritance of all of the Kingdom is yours. You become hell's worst nightmare.

> **Understand, as a child of God you have the authority of heaven in you.**

The enemy may come against you one way, but as a child of God, he will run from you in seven different ways (Deuteronomy 28:7). The enemy is confused, conflicted, and condemned in the Name of Jesus. I love that scripture because seven is the number for perfection. That means when the enemy flees in seven different ways, that is perfect confusion, a perfect defeat, and you have perfect victory.

When you say *in the Name*, that word means in the authority of... As a child of God, your authority comes from Christ. In Him, all things are held together, and without Him, nothing can stay together (Colossians 1:17). Therefore, when you proclaim something in His Name, you are proclaiming ultimate authority.

When you say *In the Name of Jesus*, it is the same as when an ambassador to a country makes a promise to that country's leaders. The ambassador does not make the promise with his own authority or name, but in the name of the country or leader he or she represents. You are an ambassador of the King of Kings and Lord of Lords. You are representing the Kingdom and King

Jesus, who is the King of Kings. You are not proclaiming by your authority but the authority of Jesus Christ.

Today, when you proclaim all this in Jesus' Name, realize you are walking in the authority of the Creator of ALL you are in. Do not take credit for the proclamation, but say out loud whose authority in which you come. *I come in the Name of Jesus Christ, the Son of the Living God, the Alpha and Omega, the bright and morning star, the strong tower, the lamb of God who takes away the sin of the world, the risen Lord, the Way, the Truth, and the Life.*

# The Amen

"FOR ALL OF GOD'S PROMISES HAVE BEEN FULFILLED IN CHRIST WITH A RESOUNDING "YES!" AND THROUGH CHRIST, OUR "AMEN" (WHICH MEANS "YES") ASCENDS TO GOD FOR HIS GLORY." 2 CORINTHIANS 1:20

"Amen is not the end of a prayer, it just gets us ready to go to the next level." —Gary Busey, Actor

## Amen

*Amen* is the last word you proclaim each day in the believer's proclamation. It is fitting and proper that you end with it. The word means so be it. Every time you say *amen*, it is a declaration that all the prior statements are so. It is a proclamation stating this is how things have been, are, and will be.

The word *amen* is a most incredibly powerful word. It is known as the best-known word in human speech. It was transliterated from Hebrew into the Greek of the New Testament and later into Latin. It is quite practically a universal word for all languages. The word is directly and almost identical to the Hebrew word for *believe* (amam). When you shout out at the end of the Believer's Proclamation, AMEN, you are literally saying, "BELIEVE"!

What an amazing proclamation. *Amen* is an expression of absolute trust and confidence! Jesus does not speak or say it; *it is spoken by you.* Jesus has spoken over you and promised all that you have proclaimed. These are the promises of God. You are the proclaimer of belief. You are the one who confidently, with absolute trust, says so be it, this is truth, this is sure, and I am most confident!

## Agree

Ending a prayer, or proclamation with *Amen* is not just a tradition or a ritual. When someone prays, preaches, or proclaims, you respond with AMEN. It is expressing belief and trust, a complete and total confidence in what is being spoken. You agree by saying it. Therefore, you make the words spoken your own. They become your belief, your prayer, your proclamation. When you connect, *In Jesus' Name* with *Amen,* you are saying, *I absolutely, positively, with complete confidence trust, believe and agree!*

Agreement is powerful. Jesus said, if even two of you agreeing on anything, in my name (in the name of Jesus) it will happen (Matthew 18:19). Each week, we proclaim the Believer's Proclamation together in our services, before the sermon. When we say Amen together, there is a power that is released in the invisible that influences the visible. When you and your spouse proclaim these statements each morning before you go to work, or as a family before your children head out to school, there is an open heaven that is established over your family no matter where you go or what you face.

Agreement between believers gets the Father's attention and He goes into action. It is the state of unity, being in one accord or like-mindedness. Agreeing and aligning yourself with the proclamation puts you in the same place as the 120 in the upper room on the day of Pentecost, when they were all in "one accord" (Acts 2). The spirit of God falls on those who agree, according to His Word. Divine power is poured out and supernatural events begin to occur.

Agreement brings synergy. Synergy is what happens when different things or people come together and the outcome is greater than the sum of each individually. The outcome of agreement is synergy; it is multiplication. You and your spouse, family, team, or church agreeing together brings about an outcome that is greater than everyone adding who and what they are. The results are multiplied beyond our wildest imagination (Ephesians 3:20).

## Absolute

There is nothing more powerful in your life than absolute belief. This is why this proclamation is called the Believer's Proclamation. Without belief, there can be no action. Your actions are determined by your belief. When you say Amen, you are igniting your actions, behavior, and course for your day, week, month, and year. You can effectively plan for what is to come. This is absolute surety, absolute faith, absolute belief.

Many people in the world want to remove being absolute and replace it with being relative. In other words, they believe there can be no absolutes in any situation. All things are relative to the circumstances or person. God is not a relative God, and neither are His children. When you say the Amen, you are declaring an absolute. He is not God for only those who believe, He is God for all. His ways are not only the ways for those who follow, they are the ways for all.

Absolute living is freeing because you realize that God is in control and He will guide your life. When doors shut, you get rejected, and the valley seems excessively dark and deep and you will continue with confidence because you know what God shuts cannot be open and what God opens cannot be shut.

When you absolutely believe you are a child of God, there will be meetings, relationships, opportunities, and doors that are acceptable and others that are not. You will know the difference because of your absolute belief. The Amen is the end of the proclamation. It is the statement made to confirm there is nothing more that needs to be said or proclaimed. Now action begins, results begin, what has been hidden is revealed.

## Activation

There is a time for words and there is a time for action. Once you have proclaimed what you believe, go out and act like it. Behave like you have faith to move mountains. Make decisions like your foundation is the Word of God. Talk like you have creative confidence and always have the attitude that matches the attitude of Jesus Christ.

Once you enter your day, you live what you have proclaimed. You activate the faith within you and

> **The word *Amen* activates your faith.**

begin each conversation, duty, meeting, project, assignment on the foundation of what you have proclaimed…your faith moves mountains, your future is out of this world, your foundation is the word of God, your walk is sure, your talk confident, your attitude Christlike, and your favor is divine.

No matter what happens in your day. No matter what the report from the doctors say. No matter how much money you have or do not have. You have said Amen. The valley may seem deep and dark. The mountain may seem too high and the tree too rooted to move. But just one action in faith. One word in belief. One decision in line with the Word of God. One moment in the right attitude and Your Father in Heaven will come flooding in with exactly what is needed in your life.

**Simply proclaim and invoke the Amen and live your life!!!**

# The Challenge

## THE NINETY-DAY BELIEVER'S PROCLAMATION CHALLENGE

The Ninety-Day Believer's Proclamation Challenge is designed to get the teachings and principles of the Word of God into your heart. This is an important aspect of the believer's life, the principle of memorization and recitation. When confronted with the confusion and difficulties of life, David wrote these words: "How does a young man keep his ways pure? By keeping them according to the Word of God" (Psalm 119:9).

David later wrote: "Your word I have hidden in my heart, so I won't sin against you" (Psalm 119:11). Do not leave the Word of God in your phone, or on the pages in a book; place the Word in your heart. As you face the day, those words will become your strength and your light. When you face a difficult temptation, you will have the strength of the Word of God flowing through your mind. You will not scurry around trying to find the Bible verse that gives strength for your current circumstance. The scripture will come flooding through your mind just like it did for the young man I told you about in the introduction...

When faced with uncertainty, confusion, or the lack of understanding, the Word of God becomes a light to reveal God's wisdom and knowledge. When you have hidden the Word in your heart (memorized it), you will have a built-in flashlight for those dark days.

Several years ago, I purchased my first smartphone. Several months later, I was with someone who had the same model. It was getting dark and we were in a parking lot and I was looking for my keys. He pulled out his phone, and with a couple of taps on the screen, what I thought was only the flash for the built-in camera became a flashlight. I looked at him and asked, "How did you do that?" He took my phone and tapped the same way on the screen and behold, my camera flash become a flashlight. For months I had had the light in my pocket. I had never accessed it because I didn't know my phone was capable of that.

I asked my friend how he knew the phone could become a flashlight. He replied, "I read the instruction manual." Wow, there it was. He didn't carry the instruction manual with him, he just remembered what it said to do when things got dark. He hid the words of the instruction manual in his knowledge (heart) for just the right time.

The point is, we have an instruction manual for life. David said, "Your Word is a lamp to my feet and a light to my path." The lamp is the Bible, the Word of God. If we do not study the words in the manual and hide them in us, when it gets dark, confusing, difficult, or disastrous, we will not know that what we have with us, the Light (Word) of God, is the light that will bring revelation and understanding.

# Here is the challenge I have for you today.

- **Memorize the Believer's Proclamation**

  **Today**, I am a **Child** of God.

  I have **Faith** to Move Mountains,

  **Favor** from the King of Kings,

  And a **Future** that is out of this world.

  My **Foundation** is the Word of God.

  My **Walk** is sure,

  My **Talk** is Confident,

  My **Attitude** is like Christ's.

  Today, I will **Hear** the Word of God.

  Today, I will **Do** the will of God.

  Today, I will be **Convicted**, **Challenged**, and **Changed**

  In Jesus' Name—**Amen**!!!

- **Commit to reciting the Believer's Proclamation every morning for ninety days.**

**You might proclaim it:**

- Before you get out of bed
- When you are in the shower
- When you leave for work


- Recite it with your spouse
- Recite it with your children
- Recite it as a family


- **Complete the Believer's Proclamation Bible Study (Order Here: childofgodbook.com)**

- **Scripture Memory**

Memorize the corresponding Bible verse for each line of the Believer's Proclamation. I have listed the corresponding scriptures below in various translations. Choose the translation that best suits you for memorization.

### Believe — 1 John 5:5 (NLT)

And who can win this battle against the world? Only those who believe that Jesus is the Son of God.

### Today — 2 Corinthians 6:2 (NLT)

For God says, "At just the right time, I heard you. On the

day of salvation, I helped you." Indeed, the "right time" is now. Today is the day of salvation.

### Child — 1 John 5:1 (NLT)

Everyone who believes that Jesus is the Christ has become a child of God.

### Faith — Matthew 17:20 (NLT)

"You don't have enough faith," Jesus told them. "I tell you the truth, if you had faith even as small as a mustard seed, you could say to this mountain, 'Move from here to there,' and it would move. Nothing would be impossible."

### Favor — Psalm 84:11 (NIV)

For the Lord God is a sun and shield; the Lord bestows favor and honor; no good thing does He withhold from those whose walk is blameless.

### Future — Ecclesiastes 6:10 (NLT)

Everything has already been decided. It was known long ago what each person would be. So there's no use arguing with God about your destiny.

### Foundation — 2 Timothy 3:16,17 (NASB)

All Scripture is inspired by God and profitable for teaching, for reproof, for correction, for training in righteousness; so that the man of God may be adequate, equipped for every good work.

### Walk — Psalm 18:33 (NLT)

He makes me as surefooted as a deer, enabling me to stand on mountain heights.

### Talk — Proverbs 18:20 (NLT)

Wise words satisfy like a good meal; the right words bring satisfaction.

### Attitude — Philippians 2:5 (NLT)

You must have the same attitude that Christ Jesus had

### Hear — Luke 11:28 (NLT)

Jesus replied, "But even more blessed are all who hear the word of God and put it into practice."

### Do — Ephesians 6:6 (NLT)

Try to please them all the time, not just when they are watching you. As slaves of Christ, do the will of God with all your heart.

### Convicted — John 16:8 (NLT)

And when He comes, He will convict the world of its sin, and of God's righteousness, and of the coming judgment.

### Challenged — James 1:12 (NLT)

God blesses those who patiently endure testing and temptation. Afterward they will receive the crown of life that God has promised to those who love him.

### Changed — Romans 12:2 (NLT)

Don't copy the behavior and customs of this world, but let God transform you into a new person by changing the way you think. Then you will learn to know God's will for you, which is good and pleasing and perfect.

**Jesus' Name — Philippians 2:9-11 (NLT)**

Therefore, God elevated Him to the place of highest honor and gave Him the name above all other names, that at the name of Jesus every knee should bow, in heaven and on earth and under the earth, and every tongue declare that Jesus Christ is Lord, to the glory of God the Father.

**Amen — 2 Corinthians 1:20 (NIV)**

For no matter how many promises God has made, they are "Yes" in Christ. And so through Him the "Amen" is spoken by us to the glory of God.

Each morning recite the Scripture for the week of the Bible study you are in after reciting the proclamation.

# Remember,

## Live everyday as a Child of God

# About The Author

Dr. J Calaway has been part of the leadership team at The Gate (a multi-site, multi-ethnic church in northwest Indiana) for the past three decades and has served as Lead Minister for 25+ years. He founded InnerMission, a 501c3 non-profit organization that seeks to make vision a reality by partnering churches and communities together. J has served on a number of different community and religious boards, both local and trans local. He has his Doctorate in Organizational Leadership. J and his wife Vicki have three grown children, five grandkids, and live in Chicago area.

# Resources

More Resources by Dr. J Calaway:

## Lead with Diligence

Becoming the Leader People want to Follow

The Power of a Question

jcalaway.com

www.ingramcontent.com/pod-product-compliance
Lightning Source LLC
Chambersburg PA
CBHW052031070526
44584CB00016B/1992